Priesthood, Pastors, Bishops

Public Ministry for the Reformation and Today

D0029488

Timothy J. Wengert

Fortress Press
Minneapolis

PRIESTHOOD, PASTORS, BISHOPS
Public Ministry for the Reformation and Today

Copyright © 2008 Fortress Press, an imprint of Augsburg Fortress. All rights reserved. Except for brief quotations in critical articles or reviews, no part of this book may be reproduced in any manner without prior written permission from the publisher. Visit http://www.augsburgfortress.org/copyrights/ or write to Permissions, Augsburg Fortress, Box 1209, Minneapolis, MN 55440.

Cover image courtesy of the Pitts Theology Library, Candler School of Theology, Emory University. Used by permission.
Cover design: Laurie Ingram
Book design: James Korsmo

Scripture quotations are from the New Revised Standard Version Bible, copyright © 1989 by the Division of Christian Education of the National Council of the Churches of Christ in the USA. Used by permission. All rights reserved.

Library of Congress Cataloging-in-Publication Data

Wengert, Timothy J.
  Priesthood, pastors, bishops : public ministry for the Reformation and today / by Timothy J. Wengert.
     p. cm.
  Includes index.
  ISBN-13: 978-0-8006-6313-1 (alk. paper)
  1. Lutheran Church—Doctrines. 2. Priesthood, Universal. 3. Church work—Lutheran Church. 4. Clergy. 5. Pastoral theology—Lutheran Church. I. Title.
  BX8065.3.W46 2008
  262'.1241—dc22
                                                              2008007893

The paper used in this publication meets the minimum requirements of American National Standard for Information Sciences—Permanence of Paper for Printed Library Materials, ANSI Z329.48-1984.

Manufactured in the U.S.A.
12   11   10   09   08   1   2   3   4   5   6   7   8   9   10

Contents

CONCORDIA UNIVERSITY LIBRARY
PORTLAND OR 9721

PREFACE

This book has two goals: (1) to unlock for English-speaking readers some of the most important sources surrounding questions of the public office of ministry in the early stages of the Lutheran movement (1520–1545) and (2) to show some ways in which the reformers' approaches to these problems may illumine our own. One problem with much of the present-day debate, as the reader will discover, is that issues from other centuries have deeply colored the interpretation of documents produced by Martin Luther and Philip Melanchthon and, in some cases, prevent us from understanding fully what their intent was and how they may be best used today. Another serious problem is simply our ignorance of the historical record and its most important texts.

When we return to these sources and read them afresh, the Reformation's exciting vision of the public ministry comes to life. Here we discover, not a disjunction between the so-called priesthood of all believers and the ordained, but the unity of the body of Christ, in which all have callings appropriate to their gifts. Here we find that the public ministers of the Word are made transparent by that very Word to bear witness in public in the Christian assembly as servants of that Word. Here we receive permission to cherish the office of oversight (bishops) in our churches and to vest bishops with proper authority in the gospel.

The chapters of this book arose from presentations requested by various groups in the church. The first two chapters began with a request by then Bishop Rembo who, as a member of the Liturgical Institute at Valparaiso University, had approached me to give a paper on the priesthood of all believers in the spring of 2005. What began as a simple exercise of gathering Luther quotes turned into full-fledged detective work as I struggled to discover when the term was invented (not by Luther but in the nineteenth century!) and how the concept in Luther's thought came to be completely reframed by later Lutheran divines. The resulting paper and later article examined both the myth of the priesthood of all believers and the original concept that Luther developed in the 1520s and used throughout his career.[1] The results of this research may finally free the nonordained to exercise their proper offices in the church and, at the same time, make clearer the purpose of the public office of ministry. There is neither laity nor clergy in the church, only baptized Christians serving within different God-given offices.

The third chapter, on the public office of ministry, came from a request by the bishops of the Evangelical Lutheran Church in America to several teachers of the church to examine the question of "lay licensure" (as it is sometimes called) for providing a ministerial presence in smaller congregations across the church. Like my fellow theologians Maria Erling, Thomas Schattauer, and Sarah Hinrichs, who all worked independently from one another, I, too, argued that people who are regularly engaged to provide the Word and sacraments to congregations should not be denied the outward sign of ordination, even if the terms of their callings remain more restricted. For this book, I have expanded chapter three to include more in-depth looks at Article 5 and Article 14 of the Augsburg Confession, originally in material that comprised the fourth and fifth chapters.

The last two chapters started with a request from the Ecumenical Institute in Strasbourg, France, to participate in a consultation on the office of bishop in churches of the Lutheran World Federation. I gave a broad historical introduction to the problem of bishops, based especially on my work with Philip Melanchthon and his comments in Article 28 of the Augsburg Confession, in the defense of that article from the Apology, and in the Treatise on the Power and Primacy of the Pope. I concluded that Lutherans have always understood oversight (*episkopé*) as a God-given part of the church's good order and that they have treasured the bishops' right to ordain as an important and deeply cherished, albeit humanly designed, part of such good church order, a definite blessing to the church except under the most extreme of circumstances when bishops demonstrate out and out contempt for the gospel.

These three general subject areas (our common spiritual priesthood, the public office of ministry, and episcopal oversight) first came together shortly after Easter 2007 in speeches presented to the pastors and rostered leaders in the South Dakota Synod of the Evangelical Lutheran Church in America. The warm reception I received there and the various requests for more information about the topics led me to consider bringing them together into this small book. Moreover, the widespread use of the online version of my article on the priesthood of all believers and the positive response I received from students in my course on the Lutheran Confessions at the Lutheran Theological Seminary at Philadelphia and from others throughout the church also encouraged me to work these presentations into a book. I have also been motivated by what I would judge has been inadequate historical and textual work on this subject, which may inadvertently be misleading some people to repeat the errors in judgment of the past. Perhaps this collection of essays can help the church to a fuller appreciation of the Reformation understanding of these topics, as it struggles to strengthen its mission in the world today. I am also especially grateful to Professor Robert Kolb of Concordia Seminary, St. Louis, for reading the manuscript and for making many helpful suggestions, and to the Rev. Martin Lohrmann for his work on the index.

Some potential readers may bristle at some of the conclusions and suggestions in this book. They are invited to consider again the historical record and the ways it has been subject to misuse in the church—not only by this scholar but also by well-intentioned, pious folks in the past, who have been only too happy to read their own solutions to later problems into Luther's and Melanchthon's work. Despite the objections of some self-appointed protectors of the laity, it seems clear to me that the public office of ministry is most under fire and most open to misunderstanding in our own day. We do well to consider the God-given authority of that office as one of God's greatest gifts to the whole church, an office established by Christ for one purpose only: public service to the word of God (aural and visible), a Word that puts to death the old and brings to life the new; a Word that at the end of this age ushers in the New World of forgiveness, life, and salvation; a Word spoken by Christ's servants to the world to make, strengthen, and gather believers.

This is not to say that the public office of ministry is not sometimes abused or that there are no bishops and other leaders in the church who, by their preaching, teaching, and leading, are not evangelical, that is, centered on this very gospel. However, in order fully to appreciate the abuse of an office, one must first establish what properly defines it. It is this task of definition that belongs to the heart of this book, as it examines some of the sources the Lutheran reformers used to redesign both the unity of all Christians and the offices of proclamation of the gospel and church oversight.

I dedicate this book to my pastor and partner, the Reverend Ingrid Fath Wengert, whose life teaches me each day about her remarkable calling, and to our pastor/bishop, the Reverend E. Roy Riley Jr., who married us and whose ministry also witnesses to the gospel of Christ.

Timothy J. Wengert
Completed in Philadelphia on June 14, 2007, the commemoration of the Cappadocian bishops, pastors, and theologians of the church: Basil of Caesarea, Gregory of Nyssa, and Gregory of Nazianzus.

Abbreviations

Ap	The Apology of the Augsburg Confession
BC 2000	*The Book of Concord.* Edited by Robert Kolb and Timothy J. Wengert. Minneapolis: Fortress Press, 2000.
BSLK	*Die Bekenntnisschriften der evangelischlutherischen Kirche,* 10th ed. Göttingen: Vandenhoeck & Ruprecht, 1986.
CA	The Augsburg Confession
LW	*Luther's Works* [American Edition]. Edited by Jaroslav Pelikan and Helmut T. Lehmann. 55 vols. St. Louis: Concordia; Philadelphia: Fortress Press, 1955–1986.
RGG	*Religion in Geschichte und Gegenwart.* Edited by K. Galling. 7 vols. 3rd ed. Tübingen, 1957–1965.
SA	The Smalcald Articles
SC	The Small Catechism
TPPP	Treatise on the Power and Primacy of the Pope
TRE	*Theologische Realenzyklopädie.* 36 vols. Berlin: De Gruyter, 1977–2004.
WA	*D. Martin Luthers Werke: kritische Gesamtausgabe.* Part 1: [*Schriften*]. 60 vols. Weimar: Böhlau, 1883–1983.
WA Br	*D. Martin Luthers Werke: kritische Gesamtausgabe.* Part 4: *Briefwechsel.* 18 vols. Weimar: Böhlau, 1930–1985.
WATR	*D. Martin Luthers Werke: kritische Gesamtausgabe.* Part 2: *Tischreden.* 6 vols. Weimar: Böhlau, 1912–1921.

CHAPTER I

THE PRIESTHOOD OF ALL BELIEVERS
AND OTHER PIOUS MYTHS

Alice laughed. "There's no use trying," she said: "one CAN'T believe impossible things." "I daresay you haven't had much practice," said the Queen. "When I was your age, I always did it for half-an-hour a day. Why, sometimes I've believed as many as six impossible things before breakfast."

Lewis Carroll, *Alice in Wonderland*

Six impossible things before breakfast! This famous Lewis Carroll quotation from *Alice in Wonderland* might well serve as the subtitle for this chapter, which began with an invitation to speak about Luther's understanding of the priesthood of all believers. Using the latest technology (the critical Weimar edition of Luther's works in digital form online), I set off to see what Luther had said and immediately ran into the Queen of Hearts. There were no references to this phrase anywhere in Luther's own writings—that is to say, *Das allgemeine Priestertum aller Gläubigen* (the common priesthood of all believers) in all of its Latin and German permutations, was nowhere to be found in Luther's writings.[1]

Although the editors of Luther's works discuss this category all over the Weimar edition, Luther himself never used the term. In fact, one of the earliest serious discussions of the category as presently understood, though not the term itself, came 150 years after Luther, in 1675, when Philip Jakob Spener penned his lengthy preface to a new printing of the sermons of Johannes

1

Arndt. In what became the manifesto of Lutheran pietism, *Pia desideria*, Spener pleaded for "the establishment and diligent practice of the Spiritual Priesthood."[2] Here, Spener used the term precisely in the way Luther had not: as a designation for part of the body of Christ, the so-called laity.

In their discussion of the priesthood of all believers published in the respected German reference work *Theologische Realenzyklopädie*, Harald Goertz and Wilfried Härle assume that Luther invented the category and argue that Spener's and Luther's understandings were the same.[3] Yet 150 years before the article in the *Theologische Realenzyklopädie* and 150 years after Spener, comments by Johann Hinrich Wichern (in connection with the Hamburg church struggle of 1839–1840) indicate that, for him, the concept came from Spener. Wichern called for a renewal of the proclamation of the priesthood of all believers from Spener's heart and mouth.[4] In fact, Spener was the first to politicize the concept and apply it to the laity, reinforcing the very division between clergy and laity that, as we shall see, Luther was trying to overcome. Spener's redefinition of the concept even contrasts to earlier usage among orthodox Lutheran theologians. For example, John Gerhard, in his sermons on 1 Peter, also wrote of a spiritual priesthood, but not in the sense that Spener used the term, as a designation for the laity, but rather as the designation of all baptized Christians.[5]

By the waning decades of the nineteenth century, this category had become completely ensconced in Luther studies. In his influential book *Luther und die Ordination*, Georg Rietschel wrote how Luther had little place for the ordained ministry and derived it exclusively from the priesthood of all believers.[6] He was writing especially against Theodor Kliefoth's popular *Liturgische Abhandlungen* and in favor of a congregationalist understanding of the church.[7] For Rietschel, ordination was nothing more than the transfer (*Übertragung*) of the authority of the entire priesthood of all believers to an individual. He was also arguing against Friedrich Stahl's analysis of church constitutions—an analysis directed at a still earlier defender of this (political) view of priesthood, Johann Höfling.[8] Thus, Rietschel concludes that "for Luther a particular office instituted on Christ's part is not necessary; it is much more bestowed with the completed salvation for the ordered congregation from itself."[9] The last sentence of his essay reflects its roots in pietism: "We are only true pastors when and insofar as we are living Christians."[10]

In his account of Luther's doctrine and the later nineteenth-century disputes, Harald Goertz never inquires after the origin of the term *das allgemeine Priestertum aller Gläubigen*, despite his own methodological interest in metaphor and hermeneutics.[11] Because of the failure to deal with this fundamental problem of definition and the ignorance of the nineteenth-century debate and the influence of Rietschel, works by English-speaking scholars are even less helpful.[12] Even though at least one editor of the critical edition of Luther's works objected to Rietschel's reconstruction of Luther's views on ordination—especially the mistaken theory that regular ordinations began in 1525—Rietschel's work has continued to dominate discussions of ministry among Lutherans.[13]

One of the most telling distortions of the historical record in North America came from Theodore Tappert, the translator and editor of *Pia desideria*. Tappert also edited *The Book of Concord* in 1959. There, in a footnote to Article 5 of the Augsburg Confession, Tappert insisted that this article was not to be understood clerically, implying that one should read it as a reference to the priesthood of all believers. Not only might he have misconstrued a footnote to the critical edition of the Lutheran confessions—it rejected a clericalistic but not clerical reading of the text—but he also reinforced the completely mistaken notion that the Augsburg Confession says little or nothing about the public office of ministry, despite the fact that Article 5 is expressly about "Das Predigtamt," the office of preaching. By dropping the footnote and changing the translation to reflect the actual meaning of the text for the new translation, Eric Gritsch (the translator) and the editors rectified this mistake, despite receiving angry phone calls and e-mails from pious pastors intent on preserving the politicized priesthood of all believers.[14] In fact, there is no mention of the priesthood of all believers anywhere in *The Book of Concord,* despite what Tappert and others imagined. So much for proving the necessity of laity Sundays from the Lutheran confessions![15]

This brings us to the point of the first two chapters of this book. The category of the "common priesthood of all believers," developed by seventeenth-century pietism and championed by some Luther scholars to this day, has nothing to do with Luther's own thought. In fact, once we jettison this notion and approach Luther's own statements de novo, we discover a far more revolutionary approach to Christian ministry—one that totally eliminates the distinction between the laity and clergy while at the same time giving new authority and purpose to the public office of ministry in Christ's church.[16]

The Scene of the Crime: *An den christlichen Adel* of 1520

The quickest way to unmask our mythical category is to return to the scene of the crime, Martin Luther's comments in one of his most influential treatises, usually called in English *Address to the Christian Nobility*.[17] This treatise was completed by June 23, 1520. At nearly the same time (July 1520), Luther produced another tract, *An Essay on the New Testament, That Is, on the Holy Mass*.[18] In it too, he spoke of something akin to the priesthood of all believers. There, however, he uses the word *Pfaffen* (cleric). His interest in the language problem dated back at least to 1519, when, in a letter to Georg Spalatin (dated December 18, 1519), Luther stated his uncertainty about the Latin term *sacerdotes* (sacerdotal priests), argued for no distinction between the laity and clergy except in service (*nisi ministerio*), and complained about the extra burdens imposed by Rome upon priests like Spalatin, whose actual office was no different than other, nonordained courtiers.[19] Other tracts that mention that all believers are *sacerdotes* include

Freedom of a Christian, Babylonian Captivity of the Church, Basis and Cause of All the Articles of Dr. Martin Luther [*Grund und Ursache aller Artikel D. M. Luthers*]; *On the Instituted Ministries of the Church* [*De instituendis ministris Ecclesiae*] (see chapter 2); *On Private Masses and the Ordination of Clerics* [*Von der Winckelmesse und Pffafenweihe*]; and *Psalm 110* [*Der 110. Psalm*].[20]

Actually, the full title of the 1520 tract is *To the Christian Nobility of the German Nation concerning the Improvement of the Christian "Stand"* [*Walk of Life*]. Already this final phrase in the title connotes a revolution in Christian thought, because it tells us what Luther expected to accomplish in the tract itself: "concerning the improvement of *the* Christian *Stand* [walk of life]." "Walk of life" is the mediocre rendering, used throughout the new edition of *The Book of Concord*, of that slippery German word *Stand*. It used to be translated "estate" (as in the estate of marriage or the fourth estate), but few are familiar with the English term nowadays. In fact, it is related more generally to the English word "standing," a term still used to designate those allowed to bring a case or an appeal before a court. In the Holy Roman Empire of the German Nation, that is, Luther's empire, the estates (*Stände*) were three: imperial nobility, clerical lords, and the imperial cities—that is, these three groups had standing (literally: "were allowed to stand") before the emperor.

More generally, in Luther's day, everyone knew that in the church itself there were two estates, two *Stände*, the worldly (or secular) "walk of life" and the spiritual (including priests, bishops, and monastics). Yet in the title of the tract, Luther has done a remarkable thing, namely, spoken of a single Christian estate: "des Christlichen Standes." There is no mistaking it. In other respects, Luther's open letter to the imperial princes was quite traditional, taking its place beside a host of fifteenth-century *gravamina*, as they were called.[21] However, previous "lists of complaints" about the church took the form of grievances by the one estate (the worldly) against the other (the spiritual). Luther, already in the title, has reduced the Christian *Stand*, or walk of life, to a single one.

There is a second place where the revolutionary flavor of Luther's tract becomes clear. Most other *gravamina* simply listed the problems of the church and offered certain "legislative proposals," as we might call them, to rectify the problems. Luther, on the contrary, had other fish to fry. He put his finger on the problem: not with individual shortcomings in imperial public and ecclesial life—although he later provided a list—but with the basic distinction between the worldly and spiritual estates. The Romanists, he argued in the introduction, had surrounded themselves with three walls to prevent their being attacked. First, when threatened by civil authority, they distinguished worldly and spiritual estates, placing the latter over the former. Second, when threatened by Scripture, they claimed that the pope had sole authority to interpret it. Third, when threatened by a council, they claimed that only the pope could call one. In his introduction, Luther set about to destroy these "paper walls," as he called them.

Luther's attack on the first wall contains the primary and most important proof text for the imaginary priesthood of all believers, and therefore we will spend most of our time looking at it. Already, the beginning of his attack makes it quite clear that Luther had something in mind other than our mythical category. "Someone invented the notion that the Pope, bishops, priests, and monastics are called the spiritual *Stand* [walk of life], while princes, lords, tradesmen and agricultural workers are the worldly *Stand* [walk of life]. This is a very fine gloss and hypocrisy."[22] The question, as Luther saw it, was whether or not there were two estates, walks of life, types of standing (before God), that is, *Stände*, in the Christian church and life.

Already we are put on notice that the way modern Lutherans have often fought over the public office of ministry is completely wrongheaded. On the one hand, Luther was not defending ontological change through ordination here—this is not what the word *Stand* implies at all. On the other hand, as Luther's solution to the medieval "doctrine of the two estates" (*Zwei-Stände Lehre*), to coin a phrase, is not simply a dive into modern American functionality and democracy. To make these two extremes the terms of the debate is to misconstrue completely Luther's true insight.

Luther begins his argument against this doctrine of the two estates by completely destroying the distinction in the Christian church:

> For all Christians are truly part of the spiritual walk of life [*Stand*], and among them there is no difference except because of the office [*Amt*] alone, as Paul says in 1 Corinthians 12[:12ff.], that we are all part of one body. Nevertheless each member has its own work so that it serves the others. This each person does, because we have one baptism, one Gospel, one faith and are equally Christians. For baptism, Gospel, and faith alone make a spiritual and Christian people.[23]

When the ontologists and functionalists do battle, it is by misconstruing the two most important words in this paragraph.[24] For Luther (and, for that matter, for his sixteenth-century readers), the word *Stand* did not mean "essence," and the word *Amt* did not merely describe a functionary. On the contrary, Luther's point becomes clear in his citation of 1 Corinthians 12 that we are all part of one body. This implied two things for him. First, our essence as Christians does not consist of more or less (Platonic) participation in God but in baptism, gospel, and faith alone. These things alone, not how enamored we are of a spirituality that unites us with God's being, give us standing before God and put us in the body of Christ.

Within that one body, then, we serve. Yet, to reduce service and office to "mere" functions, the authority of which is derived from the priesthood of all believers, is to miss Luther's point entirely. The fact that he used this word, "serve," means that Luther placed at the center of his understanding of offices not lordship (*Herrschaft*) but servanthood (*Dienerschaft*).[25] That is, he interpreted everything that happens in the body of Christ under the theology of the cross. Luther's theology of the cross is not a theory about Christ's crucifixion—although it has implications for how we view Christ's death. It is, instead, as he put it, the "*revelatio Dei sub contrario specie*," that is, the revelation of God under the appearance of the opposite or, in other words, God revealed in the last place people would reasonably look.[26] Thus, holding an office within the one body of Christ can never be a claim to power but is a powerful claim to weakness, to service. This is not simply a "going through the motions" or "fulfilling certain functions" or "lording it over the laity," but rather a self-emptying and a laying down of one's life. Service, understood as dying for the other, has what one might even call an ontological edge to it, since, in Aristotelian physics at any rate, the one thing that changes the "substance" or essence (*ontos*) of who we are is death.

Thus, this text cannot mean "anyone can be a pastor," but rather means, "all of us are members of the one body of Christ and individually servants to each other in our respective offices." The Protestant and pietistic misappropriation of these terms turns everything on its head and replaces service with power grabbing and the unity of Christ's body with the disunity of individualistic spirituality. As Paul Rorem of Princeton Theological Seminary once said, the democratic, American misconstrual of the priesthood of all believers means, in actuality, the priesthood of no believers.

Having said that, however, it is important to realize what Luther does insist on. By virtue of our baptism, we *are* all priests, bishops, and popes—that is to say, we are all Christians.[27] However, this did not imply for him a democratization of the Christian church or a denigration of the pastoral office. Instead, it was an attack on the papal claim that, by virtue of the power to consecrate and ordain, the pope and his bishops could create a separate, spiritual *Stand* [walk of life]. Read in this light, Luther's comments that follow make sense:

> That the pope or bishop anoints, makes tonsures, ordains, consecrates, or dresses differently from the laity, may make a hypocrite or an

idolatrous oil-painted icon, but it in no way makes a Christian or spiritual human being. In fact, we are all consecrated priests through Baptism, as St. Peter in 1 Peter 2[:9] says, "You are a royal priesthood and a priestly kingdom," and Revelation [5:10], "Through your blood you have made us into priests and kings."[28]

It is the papal claim that, by virtue of ordination, a bishop may transfer someone into the spiritual Christian estate that rouses Luther's ire. The claim itself simply makes hypocrites, or *olgotzen*, a delightful, sixteenth-century German word that means "an oil icon depicting a god." The only way anyone in Luther's day or in ours becomes Christian or spiritual is through baptism. With one stroke, Luther eliminated the laity as a separate category of Christian existence. In this sense, we are all priests, but only in the sense that the word *priest* is used here, namely, as "a Christian or spiritual human being."

Having robbed episcopal consecration of its previous authority and destroyed the "two-estate theory," Luther faced two problems: he had to explain what ordination was and he had to explain what set the public office of ministry apart from other Christian offices.[29] However, he had to do this in such a way as to prove that he was not teaching anything new in the church—a sure sign of heresy for any sixteenth-century theologian—but was merely recalling earlier church practices. Here is how he did it. He began by redefining the purpose of ordination:

> Thus, the bishop's consecration is nothing other than when he, in the place of and on behalf of the entire assembly takes someone from the general populace [*Hauffen*], who all have equal authority, and entrusts to him the exercise of this authority for the others. Just as if ten brothers, who were the children of a king and equal heirs, were to select one who would rule the inheritance for them. They are all kings and hold equal authority, but still the rule is entrusted to one. Let me say it even more clearly. If a small group of godly Christian lay persons were captured and left in the wilderness, and they did

not have among them a priest consecrated by a bishop, and they were there agreed and chose one among them—whether single or not—and they entrusted to him the office of baptizing, celebrating the Mass, forgiving sin and preaching, he would be truly a priest, as if all bishops and popes had consecrated him. From this principle we derive the notion that in an emergency any person can baptize and absolve, which would not be possible were we not all priests.[30]

Luther in no way denies the authority or office of the bishop to ordain. Instead, it is the one ordained, taken from the general populace possessing equal authority, who is entrusted by the bishop with the authority that belongs to all in the congregation. This, Luther claims, was the practice of the ancient church.[31] The example of the royal brothers is hardly far-fetched, since there were all kinds of secular power-sharing agreements among noble heirs. Yet, Luther seemed dissatisfied with this simile ("Let me say it even more clearly") and added an example that is, in fact, quite traditional indeed. Canon law recounts a story attributed to Augustine, who told of two men on a sinking ship, one a catechumen and the other a baptized Christian who had committed a grave sin. The latter baptized the former so that the former could pronounce absolution on the latter.[32] Indeed, the notion of emergency baptisms or absolutions performed by any Christian and recognized as valid by the church had an ancient and storied history. What *is* new is that Luther now applies the same rule to ordination—but only for Christians trapped in a desert and unable, by virtue of this emergency, to avail themselves of the normal order of the church. The underlying points dare not be forgotten: we are all priests by virtue of our baptism; the church must have public ministers.

Why did Luther argue this way and lift up the importance of baptism in making spiritual people? The answer comes in the next paragraphs: to assure the princes that they have the authority to intervene in ecclesiastical governance—ecclesiastical *governance* because, in the matter of publicly preaching the gospel or presiding at the Lord's Table, Luther drew the line.[33] The secular authorities may, as Christians, exercise their own office to keep order, and no one may, by virtue of the "doctrine of the two estates," claim exemption from such authority. To invent a Lutheresque simile: just as, in exercising their offices, a Christian mother may (indeed, must) suckle her baptized newborn and a Christian father may change its diapers, so Christian rulers may exercise their God-given office of governance among their fellow believers.

However, having given Christian princes authority to exercise their office among all other Christians does not mean that Luther was inviting the secular fox into the ecclesial henhouse or that there was no special office of the public ministry. In fact, immediately after introducing the role of princes, Luther shored up the authority of the pastoral office, something commentators have sometimes overlooked:

> For whatever crawls out of the baptismal font may boast about itself that it is already consecrated a priest, bishop and pope, although it is not seemly for each to exercise such an office. For, because we are all equally priests, no one dare push him or herself forward and usurp [this office] without our permission and election to do this, since we all have equal authority. For what is held in common no one may take for themselves without the community's permission and entrustment. Moreover, whenever it happens that someone is elected to such an office and then is deposed because of malfeasance, he becomes just what he was before. Therefore the priesthood should be nothing other in Christianity than an officeholder: as long as he is in [such an] office, he carries out [its duties]; where he is deposed, then he is a peasant or citizen like the others.[34]

At first blush, the text seems to strike a blow in favor of our mythical priesthood of all believers: "For whatever crawls out of the baptismal font . . . is already consecrated a priest, bishop, and pope." This would seem to settle it, were it not for two things. First, one can hear the metaphorical character of Luther's comments, since no one talks about the bishopric or papacy of all believers, and yet Luther lumped the three together.[35] Second, already in 1520, Luther realized that our baptism may consecrate us as priests but does not authorize us to exercise the pastoral office.[36] This was long before Luther had to worry about the ravers (*Schwärmer*), those self-appointed, clandestine preachers who even today insinuate themselves into churches by claiming some inner spiritual authority to teach and preach. In Luther's mind, being *equally* priests through baptism prevents, *prevents*, the very kind of power grabbing that passes for congregational autonomy or lay authority in churches today. Luther worried about usurpation of such authority "without our permission and election." Thus, he wrote: "For what is held in common no one may take for themselves without the community's permission and entrustment."[37]

Of course, what he was talking about here was the authorization to *exercise* the authority of the public office of ministry. However, in no way, shape, or form was he deriving the authority of the office itself from such authorization. Neither the community nor the officeholder possesses the authority of the office indelibly. Instead, the authority of the office rests in the office itself and in the word of God that created the office and for which Christ established the office, as we will see below.

No wonder that, in what followed, Luther attacked the Roman notion that ordination imbues the person's soul with an ontological change (*character indelibilis*). Today, however, we do well to turn Luther's critique not just against the dreams of some lovers of rapprochement with Rome but against those who would give to congregational presidents, pastors, or congregations a similar indelible character—as if any of us could claim the authority of the office for ourselves. We *hold* office, we entrust it to someone, or we allow others to do that entrusting on behalf of the whole church, but we do not possess the office or its authority, nor do we or can we create it or transfer it.

Luther's principle—a single walk of life but many offices— arose from his conviction concerning the unity of Christ's body.

Luther insisted that any multiplication of walks of life [*Stände*] in this context would imply two bodies of Christ.[38] It was this abhorrence of division in Christ's body that stood at the heart of his criticism of papal grabs for power and its fundamental denial of princely authority and office within the church. Thus, the way to employ Luther's argument today may be not simply to assert the authority of the laity (a power grab not unlike the pope's) but to insist on the church's fundamental unity:

> From this it follows that the laity, priests, princes, bishops and—as they call them—spiritual and worldly [walks of life]—truly possess basically no other distinction than that of their office [*Amt*] and work but *not* of their walk of life [*Stand*]. For they are all part of the spiritual walk of life [*Stand*]—truly priests, bishops and popes. However, they do not participate in the same, individual work, no more than is true among priests and monks themselves. This is what Paul said in Romans 12[:4ff.] and 1 Corinthians 12[:12ff.] and Peter said in 1 Peter 2[:9] (as I mentioned above), that we are all one body, with Jesus Christ as the head and each as a member. Christ does not have two bodies or two kinds of bodies—one worldly and the other spiritual. He is the one head and has one body.[39]

Precisely at this point in the argument, Luther distinguished priests and bishops from others on the basis of their unique office within Christ's body: "They are supposed to employ God's Word and the sacraments. That is their work and office." (Philip Melanchthon will use this same definition in Article 28 of the Augsburg Confession; see chapter 4.) Luther then defined the offices of others in Christ's body: secular authorities punish evil and protect the upright. "Each shoemaker, smith, farmer and the like has his own office and trade, and nevertheless all are equally consecrated priests and bishops. And each with his office or work ought to provide aid and service to the others, so that all kinds of work can be set up in a community to support body and soul, just as the members of the body all serve each other."[40] The point of all of these offices is always and only service—whether making shoes, keeping order, or administering God's word and sacraments. The mistaken notion, so prevalent in our power-hungry society and church, that being "consecrated priest or bishop" through our baptism gives each of us individually the right to preach or celebrate the Lord's Supper was the farthest thing from Luther's mind. In fact, Luther's point, as becomes clear in the very next sentences, was to buttress his own argument that the Christian magistrate (indeed, *any* magistrate) has the right and duty to punish errant priests and bishops. To support this, he used images of the unity of the body and the necessity of one member of the body to help another. Luther intended to prevent the ruin of the pastoral office by allowing the governmental officials to intervene in ecclesial governance by exercising their office of keeping order.

Luther proceeded to reduce his opponents' objections against such intervention to absurdity. If Christian princes did not have the right to intervene, "then a person should also prevent tailors, cobblers, stone masons, carpenters, cooks, waiters, farmers and all kinds of tradesmen from producing shoes, clothing, houses, food, drink—or even the payment of the church tax [*Zins*]—for the pope, bishops, priests and monks."[41] Of course, the attitude that some in our churches have regarding the punishment of those guilty of sex crimes or embezzlement may still faintly echo the old notion that the church plays by its own rules and is exempt from governmental intervention.

But notice what Luther is *not* saying. He is not saying that "carpenters, cooks and waiters" should preach; rather, he is saying that they should carry out their own God-given offices. So if someone wants to invoke Luther's understanding of the universal, spiritual priesthood properly, it should be to urge paying a higher percentage of one's salary to support the pastor or to fix the leaks in the parsonage roof. Of course, this also means that Christian clergy can never *demand* tax exemptions (special status with the IRS is simply a matter of governmental largesse, not a divine right) or insist on handling sex offenders in their own courts.

Having destroyed this first wall of separation between papacy and laity, Luther then examined the second, namely that the pope alone can interpret Scripture. Here he uses 1 Corinthians 14:30 (that one Christian should yield to another) and John 6:45 (that we are all taught by God). The papacy usurped this function of interpreter and could not use Matthew 16:19 in its favor, since the keys were given to all Christians and had to do with forgiveness of sins. Moreover, Christ prayed in the upper room not only for Peter (as in Luke 22:32) but for all the apostles and the whole church (John 17:9, 20). Luther then appealed to common sense: that there are upright Christians who understand Scripture. Why should they yield to the pope? Otherwise, the Apostles' Creed would have to be changed to, "I believe in the Pope in Rome" instead of the "Holy Christian Church."

Luther simply refused to allow the pope alone to interpret Scripture. Because Christians have one faith, one gospel, and one sacrament, all have authorization to verify and judge (*zuschmecken und urteilen*) what is correct or not in matters of faith. This means that, contrary to canon law, all Christians have authority to judge a non-Christian or an anti-Christian pope (or, we could add, a bishop or pastor or congregational president). Just as Abraham had to listen to Sarah (Genesis 21:12), who was clearly subject to the patriarch, and Balaam had to listen to his donkey (Numbers 22:28), even more so an upright Christian can upbraid an errant pope.[42] Of course, the key here is not congregational rights, but the unity of Word and sacrament and the role of true faith. It is not just any old Christian, but "*ein frommer Christ*," an upright Christian, who may correct the pope. Luther did not see or did not seem concerned about the apparent contradiction: Who determines who is upright? For Luther, this problem of jurisdiction was far less important than destroying papal hegemony over the church.

Even the third wall, constructed to allow popes alone to call councils, fell apart in Luther's eyes, since again the unity of the church and the respect for all members undermined this usurpation of power. Here, especially, Luther hearkened back to the notion of emergency (*die Not*) and the unity of Christ's body. Luther employed examples of two of the most feared things in sixteenth-century life: fire in a city and enemy attack. What sense, he asked, would it make if, when a fire broke out in a city, everyone just stood around because they did not have the mayor's authority to fight it? Indeed, everyone has the authority to sound the alarm, as in the case of a surprise attack by the enemy. It was precisely this kind of dire emergency (and not just the selfish demagoguery now plaguing the church) that Luther had in mind. His point? No one in the church has the right to cause it damage!

Thus, Luther was neither trying to attack the office of preaching and presiding nor attempting to trumpet the authority of the laity; rather, he was assailing ecclesiastical pyromaniacs of every kind—papal, episcopal, pastoral, congregational, or individual. In his view, the first question that needs answering is never "Don't laypersons have rights?" but "Where's the fire?"—that is, "Is serious damage being done to the church and its proclamation of the gospel?" In this regard, Luther's favorite Bible verse was 2 Corinthians 10:8, where Paul speaks of his authority, "which the Lord gave for building you up and not for tearing you down." For Luther, as soon as our question becomes "laity rights" or "clergy rights," only the Antichrist or his cousin wins out.

CHAPTER 2

OTHER "PROOFS" FOR THE EXISTENCE OF THE PRIESTHOOD OF ALL BELIEVERS

Less than a month after he had finished the manuscript for *An den christlichen Adel*, Luther produced a smaller piece on the Lord's Supper, in which he offered hefty critique of the sacrifice of the Mass.[1] In it, he stressed the centrality of Christ's priesthood and how we bring our praise and needs to Christ, who (according to Romans 8:34) offers us up to God (as opposed to our offering Christ to God). Our true offering occurs by faith, whether connected to the Mass or not. "Thus, it is clear that not only the priest offers the Mass but each individual in his or her own faith. This is the true priestly office through which Christ is offered up before God, which office the priest signifies with the external gestures of the Mass, and all are thus equally spiritual priests before God."[2] Again, the point is that we are all equally *spiritual* priests. In fact, the notion of a gang of such spiritual priests demanding to preside at the Lord's Supper was unthinkable to Luther.

Moreover, for Luther, the point of such priesthood was hardly power or authority in the local congregation but faith in Christ. This alone makes priests and priestesses, he wrote, using *pfaffen* (parson), not *priester* (priest), to make his point. The abstraction of these comments to a general doctrine of the priesthood of all believers—especially as a way to run congregations and turn pastors into hired guns—was the farthest thing from Luther's mind. All he was interested in doing here is proving the centrality of faith for all people at the Lord's Supper.[3]

For all of those who have faith that Christ is Pastor for them in heaven before God's face and who rely on him and through him present their prayers, praise, needs and themselves, and who do not doubt that he does this himself and offers himself for them, they take therein the Sacrament and Testament, either bodily or spiritually, as a sign of all of this and do not doubt that all sins are forgiven and that God has become a gracious, heavenly Father and prepared an eternal life. Look! All those, wherever they are, are the true priests [*pfaffen*] and hold true, proper Mass, and obtain therewith whatever they want. For faith must do all of this. Faith alone is the proper priestly office and does not allow anyone to be anything else. Thus, all Christian men are priests [*pfaffen*] and all women are priestesses [*pfeffyn*], whether young or old, lord or servant, lady or maid, learned or lay. Here there is no difference, even if faith is unequal. Then again, all who do not have such faith but instead presume that the Mass is a sacrifice to be offered up and to perform their office before God are oil painted icons of gods, hold an external mass, do not themselves know what they are doing, and "cannot please God, whom it is impossible to please without true faith," as Paul says in Hebrews 11[:6].[4]

Luther's Tract *On the Ordering of Ministries*

A final tract sometimes used to "proof text" Luther's doctrine of the priesthood of all believers is his *De instituendis ministris Ecclesiae* (*On the Instituted Ministries of the Church*).[5] This tract was written in 1523 for the Utraquist bishops of Bohemia, who, despite their relative independence from Rome, still sought from the pope confirmation of their appointments as bishop.[6] However, in his (to be sure, somewhat mistaken) account of early church life, Luther traced the development of bishops *not* from the priesthood of all believers but from the paterfamilias of Christian households.[7] The crucial thing here is that Luther was thinking *not* about a democratization of Christianity but rather that, in the absence of the preaching of the gospel in the assembly, the head of the household was to take action to read the gospel and even to baptize. Luther chose these two things because his opponents could not provide a counterargument. They permitted "the laity" to do these things. Thus, Luther was able to counsel those who must live with bad teaching to restrain themselves, since the Lord's Supper, which could not occur in the house church, was not necessary during a crisis (*sub periculum*). From a single Christian household, Luther immediately extrapolated to unity among true Christians at a wider level.[8] Here the "congregational" mode of thinking that dominates so much of pious Christian thinking nowadays is put to rest. Luther wrote of many households, a whole city, and then many cities. They are united by a domestic gospel and can live without the Supper without harming their standing as Church, since only the word of God is necessary in times of danger.

Far from undermining the public office of ministry, as has sometimes been alleged, Luther supports it in this tract and places it on a much firmer footing:

> For because this ordination was instituted by the authority of the Scriptures and then by the example and decrees of the Apostles for this purpose, namely, that it [ordination] would set in place [*instituo*] ministers of the Word among the people, therefore, I say, public ministry of the Word, by which the mysteries of God are dispensed, ought to be instituted through sacred ordination, or the reality which of all things in the Church is the highest and greatest, in which the entire power of the Ecclesiastical power consists, since without the Word nothing exists in the Church and through the Word all things exist. But to me the Papists do not dream about this ministry in their ordinations.[9]

In this passage, we see in what high regard Luther held both ordination and the public ministry, and we discover how he connected the two things. Ordination was the means of "instituting" servants of the Word. The Latin verb *instituo* means, literally, "to put in place" and, more broadly, "to establish, institute or appoint to an office." Here we see most clearly that Luther, far from eliminating the ordained ministry or making it subservient to the laity or the congregation, understood that the "public ministry of the Word" is the means by which "the mysteries of God are dispensed." There is nothing higher or greater in the church than that Word.

What Luther insisted upon in this document was the reinstatement of the consent of the people in any priestly or episcopal appointments. Here, in an even stronger way than in the previous treatments of the issue, Luther stressed the authority of God's word in establishing and defining the public office of ministry. In the rest of the tract, he contrasted the ministry of the Word over against the pseudo-office to which bishops were in his day ordained: to baptize baptismal fonts, altars, and bells rather than human souls. Moreover, they ordained priests not to preach and teach the word of God, but to stand at altars and recite innumerable private masses for the dead.

"A SACERDOTAL PRIEST IS NOT WHAT A PRESBYTER or Minister is: The former is born; the latter is made."[10] This single line, capitalized in the original, makes it clear that, when Luther used the word "priest" (Latin: *sacerdos*), he did not mean the public office of ministry (Latin: *presbyterum* or *ministrum*). We are born (through Baptism) sacerdotal priests; we are made public ministers. However, "to make" something is not to create a new kind of being (something that only happens through birth or death), but to set a particular being in an office. Here Luther contrasted the word *sacerdos* (sacerdotal priest) to the word *presbyteros* (elder, from which the English word *priest* comes) and showed that, in the New Testament only, Christ is *sacerdos* or, by extension, all baptized believers in Christ.[11] However, ordination makes elders *presbyteroi*, not *sacerdotes*.[12]

When, therefore, Luther went on to attack episcopal ordination, he did it not because he opposed ordination or the public ministry and its authority, but rather because of the myth perpetrated by such ordinations: that such people had entered or, rather, been born into a new *Stand*. Christ's priesthood was not dependent on such action and, therefore, those made priests in Christ through Baptism also did not need such things:

> For Christ was neither tonsured nor anointed with oil in order to be made a sacerdotal priest. Wherefore it is not necessary for the one following Christ to be anointed in order to be made a sacerdotal priest, but it is necessary that such a one have something completely different which, because he had it, such a one has no need of oil and tonsure. As you see that the Bishops, ordainers of such ghosts, err sacrilegiously since they make their anointing and ordaining so necessary that they deny that without them a sacerdotal priest can be made, although such a one may be the holiest person, or Christ himself.[13]

Luther then defined the duties of such sacerdotal priests as "teaching, preaching and announcing the Word, baptizing, consecrating or administering the Eucharist, absolving or binding sins, praying for others, sacrificing, and judging concerning all doctrines and spirits."[14] He then proved that each function arose from the word of God and belonged to this sacerdotal priesthood. However, rather than being proof of the authority of the priesthood of all believers over public ministers, as may seem the case, Luther insisted that the ministry of the Word in such a sacerdotal priesthood was given "to all Christians communally."[15]

By far the most difficult part of his proof comes with the Lord's Supper. With things like preaching and baptizing or even, in an emergency, forgiving sins, his opponents already agreed that the "laity," as they called it, could manage such things. However, in their minds, the Lord's Supper was a different matter altogether and was (and is!) reserved only for the Roman priests:

> The third duty is to CONSECRATE or to administer the sacred bread and wine. But here the ordained tonsured people triumph and reign, conceding this authority neither to the angels nor to the virgin Mother. But to their insane masses we say that this duty, too,

is for all communally, just as the sacerdotal priesthood [is for all]. And we assert this not on our authority but Christ's, who says in the Last Supper, "This do in my remembrance," from which Word the tonsured papists want sacerdotal priests to be made and the power of consecration to be derived. But this Word Christ said to all who were present and would be present, who would eat that bread and drink that cup. Therefore, whatever is derived from there is derived for all.[16]

The point is obvious. Luther imagined the Lord's Supper to be a communal event, involving at the same time all who do this (past, present, and future), both celebrants and recipients. By moving the action of the Supper from the consecration to the distribution, Luther had effectively recalled the church to the original intent of the meal—not as a show performed by a special breed [*Stand*] of people effective by its mere performance (*ex opere operato*) but as a meal shared in common. This, of course, would transform the one who presides from sacerdote into servant.

Later in the tract, Luther went so far as to approve a distinction made by his opponent Jerome Emser, who had insisted, in an earlier refutation of Luther, that there were two groups described in the 1 Peter text, all Christians spiritually and communally and some specially and externally.[17] After having proved that all hold in common these aspects of the sacerdotal office, Luther then returned to Emser's point and refined it:

But we have said that all these things pertain to the communal right [*ius*] of Christians. For because these things are all the communal property of all Christians (as we have proved), it is allow to no one to appear in the midst [of them] by his/her own authority and to seize for him/herself alone what belongs to everyone. You may well claim that right and exercise it where no one has a similar right. But this communally held right makes it so that one person or however many please the community are elected or accepted. These, in the place of and name of all (who have the same right), exercise these offices publicly, lest there be shameful confusion among the people of God, and some Babylon happen in the Church. "But let all things be done according to order," as the Apostle (1 Cor 14:40) taught. For it is one thing to exercise a right publicly, and another to use the right in necessity. It is not permitted to exercise [it] publicly except with the consent of the whole community or of the Church. In necessity, whoever wants may use it.[18]

This was just the point Luther made earlier to undermine the "Zwei Ständelehre" (doctrine of two estates) in *To the Christian Nobility*. There is no one, not a congregational pope, a pastoral pope, a synodical pope, or a Roman pope, who has that authority in and of himself. Instead, the office is given to all in general and requires that everyone be in agreement. For Luther, an important proof text for the public office of ministry was 1 Corinthians 14:40—the good order of the congregation and church. But he also stressed the public nature of that exercise and the importance of an emergency [*in necessitate*]. Citing 1 Corinthians 4:1, Luther called a holder of this public office a minister, servant, or steward. He summarized his arguments this way:

> Let us take our stand on this: There is no other Word of God than what is commanded to be announced to all Christians. There is no other baptism than that which any Christian can confer. There is no other memorial of the Lord's Supper than where any Christian can do what Christ instituted to do. There is no other sin than what any Christian ought to bind and absolve. There is no other sacrifice than the body of any Christian whatsoever. Only a Christian alone can pray. Only a Christian ought to judge concerning doctrines. These, however, are the signs of the sacerdotal priesthood and kingship.[19]

On the basis of these arguments, then, Luther advised the Bohemian bishops to begin to consecrate their own bishops without waiting for Rome's approval. For all of its radicality, Luther's statements define not a politicized laity but an authority for the single Christian estate, what Luther here labels a sacerdotal priesthood, while leaving room for the servanthood of the public office of ministry.[20] Moreover, his point was not to abolish the public office of ministry or derive its authority from the priesthood of all believers, but just the opposite: to empower the Bohemian bishops and clergy to act on behalf of the public ministry of the Word. Indeed, Luther did not even wish to abolish the office of bishop but merely its dependence upon a tyrannical arrangement under which they were forced to seek approval from the pope:

> "It is a new thing," they say, "and without precedent, to elect and create bishops." I respond: On the contrary, it is most ancient and approved by the examples of the apostles and their disciples, although abolished and extinguished through the papists by an opposing example and pestilential teachings. Furthermore, this must rather be so that you may reject the recent example of this plague and recall the salutary example of ancient times. Moreover, even if it were a completely new thing, nevertheless here the Word of God shall shine and command and, at the same time, the necessity of souls demands it. Again, the novelty of the thing ought not move [us] but the majesty of the Word. For, I ask, what is not new that faith does? Was it not also at the time of the Apostles a new ministry of this kind? Was it not new that Abraham offered his son? Was it not new, that the sons of Israel crossed the sea? Will it not be new for me that I will go through death into life? But the Word of God is seen in all of these things, not novelty in itself, otherwise if such novelty is enough to get in the way, then it may not ever be licit to believe any Word of God.[21]

Thus, far from overturning apostolic, historic succession among bishops, Luther sought to uphold it and revive it in the face of papal abuse. Moreover, even if he could not prevent his argument from being labeled a novelty, Luther switched to an eschatological argument derived from the word of God itself: faith and salvation are themselves always new and renewing. Thus, rescuing the office of bishop in this matter is similarly an eschatological good thing grounded in God's ever-renewing word. Moreover, Luther also did not imagine doing this "new thing" in anything but an old way. Just as the early house churches relied on the paterfamilias, so Luther instructed the Bohemian church to "impose upon them the hand of those who were more prominent among you, confirm and commend them to the people and to the Church or the whole community."[22]

Applying the "Common Priesthood" in Luther and Beyond

What difference does this make? Is this not mere playing with words? Can we not still insist upon the time-honored category of the priesthood of all believers (it rolls off the tongue so easily) as a way of understanding Luther's thought? Of course, we would have not ventured so far into Luther's writings if the answer were yes. Instead, jettisoning this nineteenth-century construct transforms the view of Luther's later thought and, at the same time, our view of contemporary understandings of ministry.

ON THE COUNCILS AND THE CHURCHES

In 1914, Karl Drescher produced volume 50 of Luther's works in the Weimar edition, which included Luther's most sophisticated treatise on the church, *On the Councils and the Churches*.[23] This volume, overseen by Otto Clemen and, more directly, by Ferdinand Cohrs, whose work on Luther's catechisms and other early Reformation catechisms is unexcelled, includes a useful introduction to the piece itself. In this introduction, the editors tie the third section of Luther's tract to the concept of the priesthood of all believers.[24] In contrast to Luther's earlier writing *To the Christian Nobility*, the editors write, Luther invoked not the priesthood of all believers, but rather the authority of Scripture itself.[25] A fine explanation, if Luther were working with such a concept as the priesthood of all believers in the earlier tracts! However, if, as we have argued, he was not, then a new sense of the unity of Luther's thought on this question emerges.

Indeed, in the third section of his tract *On the Councils and the Churches*, Luther expressed in fuller form a Reformation ecclesiology that he had already developed almost twenty years earlier. He insisted that the Greek word for church, *ekklesia*, meant simply "an assembly of people." The important word in defining "church" theologically, therefore, rested in its adjectives. Church was not the Roman structure of popes and bishops, it was not any assembly of people, and it surely was not a building, as people commonly said in Luther's day and say in ours. Instead, it was a holy assembly made holy through the activity of the Holy Spirit, who forgives sins, creates faith, and restores new life.[26] Moreover, church did not just consist of the apostles of bygone days but also included in its assembly not only present-day believers but all believers until the end of the world, wherever Christ works to redeem and the Holy Spirit works to make us holy and bring us to life. Thus, according to Luther, the holy Christian people are truly universal (*catholica*) and not restricted to one place or time. Wherever the Holy Spirit, using God's word, goes about the business of killing the old creature of sin and enlivening the new creature of faith, there is church.

To recognize this holy Christian assembly, God provided it with certain marks, expanded here by Luther from the simple two (Word and sacraments) to seven: Word, Baptism, Supper, the keys of absolution, ministry, prayer (including catechism), and cross.[27] Throughout this section, Luther contrasted the holiness given by the Holy Spirit through these marks and means of grace to the external holiness of the papal religion of his day.

However, it is in the fifth mark, ministry, where we can most clearly hear not a break between the "old Luther," who was grumpy and clericalistic, and the bold, happy, pietistic "young Luther," but the very continuity in thought that defined both a single Christian walk of life (*Stand*) and a variety of offices (*Ämter*).[28] In 1520, Luther had emphasized the single *Stand*; he concentrated on the public office. Thus, he began the section with a statement that (on the surface) directly contradicted his earlier position:

> Fifth, one recognizes the church externally in that it ordains or calls servants of the church or has offices that it fills. For one must have bishops, pastors or preachers, who publicly and specially distribute, offer, and practice the above-mentioned four things or holy objects, because of and in the name of the church but much more because of the institution of Christ, as St. Paul says in Ephesians 4[:11], "He gives gifts to people." He gave some to be Apostles, Prophets, Evangelists, Teachers, Rulers, etc.[29]

He then appealed to the sense of order and to 1 Corinthians 14:40, as above, but now to emphasize the necessity of the public office.[30] So convinced was Luther of the existence of this mark of the church that he had to explain why some people (women, children, and the mentally challenged) would naturally be excluded from this office.[31] (As is often the case in Luther's arguments, he introduced this argument only *because* he realized that up until then he had offered no specific argument why especially women should be excluded.)[32] He further had to explain why the Lutheran church had no prophetic or apostolic offices, while the Roman church, in the person of the pope, did. He argued that the pope and his followers were more likely apostles of the devil because they did not know as much about Scripture as a seven-year-old girl (perhaps he had his own Magdalena in mind).[33] Apostles and prophets will continue to exist in the church until the world's end, even if they have other names. For Luther, the point was never the worthiness or honor of the officeholders but the Word of God to which they bear witness. After a long tirade attacking the pope's strictures against married clergy,[34] Luther turned to other marks of the church, but not before concluding: "Where you see such offices or office holders, there you may know for a certainty that the holy Christian people must be there. For the Church cannot exist without such bishops, pastors, preachers and priests.

And, again, they cannot exist without the church; they must be together."[35] They must be together. This is what Luther had seen that the church of his day lacked in 1520; nineteen years later, the need was still the same.

FINDING OUR WAY IN THE TWENTY-FIRST CENTURY

Several years ago, during the debate over the proposed agreement between the Evangelical Lutheran Church in America and the Episcopal Church, "Called to Common Mission," I was asked to address the Southeast Pennsylvania Synod Assembly on how Lutherans understood the laity and the clergy. I had five minutes for each topic, immediately before and after lunch. It was my first sentence that grabbed their attention and surprised—nay, shocked—the bishop. I announced, "There are no lay voting members at this synod assembly." Of course, by the time I announced after lunch that there were also no clergy voting members, no one was listening.

The fact remains. We are, first and foremost, members of a church—that is, the *Christian* church—in which, standing before God, there are no lay or clerical members anywhere. There are not two different estates of Christians with two different standings before God. There is only one body of Christians, all of whom are called to serve one another with their gifts where they are. The elimination of all essential differences between clergy and laity, however, does not lead to a haughty dismissal or denigration of the pastoral office (as sometimes occurred in pietism). Rather, as Luther realized that, by erasing this distinction, we all become members of the same, single, united body of Christ. Anything that anyone does to undermine that unity—in the name of either clerical or lay power—contradicts directly Luther's concern.

Second, this unity of Christ's body—a gift of the Holy Spirit—does not mean uniformity of action. Each of us is called to serve with our own distinctive gifts. Shoemakers can make shoes; congregational leaders can lead and administer; and pastors can (and must) preach and preside. The wholesale usurpation by officeholders in one office of the duties and responsibilities in another—except in the case of a true emergency (which is then hardly usurpation)—has no place in the church, despite its popularity among some demagogues today. There is good order in our Lutheran churches today. Congregational leaders do not belong in the pulpit; the pastor is not above the law—whether exercised in the congregation or synod or by the state. Again, the point for Luther is unity—in this case, the unity in diversity that any healthy body demonstrates.

Even more centered upon unity is a third point. The sacerdotal priesthood belongs to Christ alone, who through faith shares it *in toto* with the whole church—Baptism, Supper, preaching, absolution, prayer, suffering. You see, the marks of the church in 1539 are the marks of this sacerdotal priesthood in 1523. Because of this, no one can usurp the public function of this priesthood to himself or herself. As long as we peer over the fence and imagine that only Rome or the Roman priesthood is guilty of this, we will miss the most egregious practices in our own backyards. Every time there is a vacancy in a parish, some congregational leader thinks God (or at least the bishop) has died and left him or her in charge. Bishops and district presidents are often elected on the basis of charm or power politics and not on the basis of their fidelity to the proclamation of the gospel! Pastors and congregations imagine that they alone define church and spurn the advice, counsel, and admonition of other congregations, pastors, bishops, or leaders. Worse yet, pastors think their calling is to do everything except exercise the public office of ministry. It is now the latest thing to jettison Word, Baptism, Supper, absolution, prayer, and—above all else—suffering from the sacerdotal estate we all share and from the office of pastor to which some of us are called. How can the church grow when the marks of the church, the priesthood, and the public office are abandoned? Such is not "church growth," but church shrink.

The Augsburg Confession states succinctly that no one may exercise the public office without a proper call, and for Luther that call includes approval by all involved. But the point is less who is involved in calling as it is in what builds up the church. In fact, Luther measured everything in terms of unity and, to use an old word, edification. We are on Earth to build one another up in unity, not to insist upon our rights or grab the office of others or run them through the mud.

Fourth, there is the issue of Baptism, preaching, and the Lord's Supper. A graduate student recently told me the story of his vacation in Montana, where he and his family visited a congregation when the pastor was away for a synod function. Without any explanation, some laypersons climbed into the pulpit and spoke and then led the congregation in the celebration of the Lord's Supper. Where was the emergency? Where was the pastor? Now, to be sure, even when we do stupid things, God still manages to use our broken words and bad form. But what bothered my student—and me—was not that, from time to time, in certain circumstances (whether quite at what I would define as the level of emergency or not), someone other than the one called to public ministry may be called upon to do these things in a particular place. Rather, what bothered us was the complete lack of explanation. It was as if what that pastor did in that congregation was just a job, easily done by anyone, or as if the pastor's "real" job had nothing to do with the public Christian acts of "bath, table, Word, and prayer" but with other things. It is hard to imagine what those things might be. But perhaps when the pastor is not sure about his or her office and simply wants to be everyone's friend, then congregational members become confused as well.

Part of the problem is that few recognize the difficulty of performing the public office of ministry well. Certainly, if I were being wheeled into an operating room and a janitor at the hospital came up to me and announced that my heart surgeon was on vacation and he was taking her place, I think I would run away as fast as my wobbly knees could carry me. It is just as much an art to perform a triple bypass as it is to recognize the distinction between law and gospel in the biblical text and to preach it well. Of course, these days, in some corners of the church, even reading Scripture, let alone preaching on it, has become passé. So perhaps in those so-called churches it really does not matter who presides.

There are, of course, emergencies, in which a respected, well-trained member of a congregation may be called upon to comfort the faithful on a particular Sunday. Given the shortage of ordained public ministers, the number of times that that will happen in the future is bound to increase. Then, too, there are the more widespread vacancies in rural or urban areas, where synods, districts, bishops, and presidents have taken a variety of approaches to the problem. As I and others have argued elsewhere (see chapter 3, for example), such "lay" ministers are public ministers in every sense of the term—except lacking ordination itself. One wonders if, by refusing to ordain such folks, ordination has become not public attestation of a call to public ministry, but rather approval for three or four years at seminary. Although we must be concerned with the anti-intellectual bent in our society that would have janitors do the ecclesial work of theological heart surgeons, we must also be willing to acknowledge the real, public ministries of real people. They might be EMTs and need more oversight and have limited mobility, but what is that compared to the mark of the church that sets apart a person for this public office?

Finally, let us leave debates over ontology and function to Plato and John Stuart Mill. Instead, let us meditate upon these verses from Paul (Romans 12:4-5): "For as in one body we have many members, and not all the members have the same function, so we, who are many, are one body in Christ, and individually members one of another." There is one body, not two estates. There are many offices that make us interrelated to one another in service. What is the office and service of the public minister of the gospel? No matter how unworthy, Philip Melanchthon stated in the Apology, such persons, "represent the person of Christ on account of the call of the church and do not represent their own persons. . . . When they offer the Word of Christ or the sacraments, they offer them in the stead and place of Christ."[36] That service, in essence and in function, means to die for the little ones whom God has given us to serve. And *that* is the office of those called and ordained public ministers in our churches: to distribute publicly the gifts of Christ's priesthood that, through Baptism, we all share in faith, whatever our duties and offices in the church may be.

Chapter 3

The End of the Public Office of Ministry in the Lutheran Confessions

There are certain neuralgic points in the history of Christianity so deeply embedded within their own time and place that later generations, burdened with their own idiosyncratic problems, find it next to impossible to decipher them. Such is the case with the office of ministry in the Reformation and, specifically, in *The Book of Concord*. The less we demand that these documents answer our questions and the more we allow them to speak in their own context, the more likely we will hear what they have to say to us.

The Public Office of Ministry at the End of the World

In a rather grim scene from the television drama *A Hitchhiker's Guide to the Galaxy*, a variety of space aliens gather in a café at the edge of the universe to watch its final collapse. As their native galaxies slowly get snuffed out, the creatures drink their beverages and look on helplessly. The reformers' view of the public office of ministry also derives from their conviction that they are living at the end of this age. However, rather than slip into a cynical, existentialist ennui, they express undying hope. For this office, in fact, announces the beginning of new life in Christ. This "eschatological" perspective (to use the word from Greek for "end times"), which undergirds their entire theology, greatly clarifies their understanding of the public ministry.

In the Augsburg Confession, justification by faith alone (Articles 4 and 20) bears this eschatological edge. Declaring forgiveness of sin ushers the hearer into the end times and pronounces ahead of time God's judgment: "Not guilty because of Christ."[1] Moreover, this promised righteousness comes to us only through the hearing of faith—not by sight or works. Thus, in the German version of Article 4, Melanchthon links Christ's suffering for us to forgiveness, righteousness, and, most significantly, eternal life:

> Furthermore, it is taught that we cannot obtain forgiveness of sin and righteousness before God through our merit, work, or satisfactions, but that we receive forgiveness of sin and become righteous before God out of grace for Christ's sake through faith when we believe that Christ has suffered for us and that for his sake our sin is forgiven and righteousness and eternal life are given to us. For God will regard and reckon this faith as righteousness in his sight.[2]

This future-looking faith, which clings to God's promise alone, demands a public office of ministry, designated by Melanchthon in Article 5 as the *Predigtamt*.[3]

> To obtain such faith God instituted the office of preaching, giving the gospel and the sacraments. Through these, as through means, he gives the Holy Spirit who produces faith, where and when he wills, in those who hear the gospel. It teaches that we have a gracious God, not through our merit but through Christ's merit, when we so believe. Condemned are the Anabaptists and others who teach that we obtain the Holy Spirit without the external word of the gospel through our own preparation, thoughts, and works.[4]

The raison d'être for this office is the justifying Word of God itself—the visible and audible promise used by the Holy Spirit to create faith in the God who in Christ promises to act for us. The eschatological nature of this office also becomes clear in the (for Melanchthon) uncharacteristic language of the Holy Spirit producing faith "where and when he wills, in those who hear the gospel." This total reliance on God's action—the hallmark of an eschatological perspective—contrasts to the views of the reformers' opponents, who were not looking to God's future, but who were stuck in their own self-made past, trusting in their own "preparation, thoughts, and works."[5]

This end-times perspective helps explain the small amount of space devoted in the Augsburg Confession (or in *The Book of Concord* as a whole) to ordering the office of ministry. Structure is important for the sake of order, but the gospel and God's work do not finally depend on how we order things. Similarly, Martin Luther construed the eschatological heart of the Lord's Prayer in the Small Catechism by repeating that God's name is hallowed, God's kingdom comes, and God's will is done in themselves and by God.[6]

Reformation eschatology also explains the hefty attacks on the papacy's understanding of ministry throughout *The Book of Concord*. Objection to the papacy arose neither out of theological pique nor out of an abhorrence of the episcopacy or apostolic tradition but simply because, in these end times, the bishop of Rome had betrayed the gospel. This is why Luther's rejection of the papacy came in part 2 of the Smalcald Articles, which contains "articles that pertain to the office and work of Jesus Christ."[7] (It is also here that he lifted up the rule and equality of bishops.)[8] Similarly, Philip Melanchthon's Treatise on the Power and Primacy of the Pope, conceived as an appendix to the Augsburg Confession, contains an eschatological flavor. The papal usurpation of political authority in Europe and its concomitant tyranny were "monstrous errors" because they "obscure faith and the reign of Christ."[9] For Melanchthon, the characteristics of the Antichrist "clearly fit the reign of the pope" because in the end times, "he will invent doctrine that conflicts with the gospel and will arrogate to himself divine authority."[10]

In the emergency of the end times, the single most important concern for the reformers was delivering the gospel (that is, the promise of God's grace in Christ), which "is very comforting and beneficial for timid and terrified consciences."[11] Christians maintain order in the church and organize the public office of ministry for the sake of that word of comfort, which alone can stave off the chaos of the end times for troubled hearts. Thus, the gospel, and the comfort it affords, demands that someone proclaim it publicly whenever Christians need it.

Sometimes, the emergency takes quite concrete form. For Martin Luther, a midwife baptizing a baby in distress fulfilled the *public* office of ministry as surely as if she had been ordained by Peter himself. Her baptism made her a part of the general priesthood we all share, but the emergency forced upon her the public office.[12] Luther also argued that an adult, unable to find a pastor to comfort his or her conscience with the forgiveness of sins, could confess even to a child. Moreover, in that emergency, the child could pronounce forgiveness with the authority of the public office. Like the mail, the gospel's message must get through—no matter what![13]

Another Look at Article 5: The Office of Preaching Revisited

To show how deep the historical problem runs, consider once again that most curious gloss to the Augsburg Confession in both the critical edition of the text from 1930 (the BSLK) and the 1959 English translation. On the German text of Article 5, "The Office of the Ministry," as later Latin and German editions of the seventeenth century titled it, the English editor, Theodore Tappert, added this note: "This title would be misleading if it were not observed (as the text of the article makes clear) that the Reformers thought of 'the office of the ministry' in other than clerical terms." He based the comment on a note in the BSLK, which supplied proof texts and added that the German word *Predigtamt* is not to be understood clerically ("klerikal"), an assumption supposedly backed up by Luther's *Sermon on Good Works*, which puts the preaching office on par with marriage and governing authorities, and by his *Confession* of 1528.[14] The note concludes with a reference to the work of Ferdinand Kattenbusch (1851–1935).[15] This scholar, known for his work on Albrecht Ritschl's correspondence as well as on the creeds, reflected on the raging nineteenth-century debate among Lutherans over church and ministry that had already been simmering among pietist and orthodox Lutheran theologians in the eighteenth century, exacerbated by the Prussian Union of 1817 and the separation of church and state during the Weimar Republic.[16]

In fact, Kattenbusch gives no proof for the assertion that the word *Predigtamt* is not "clerical." In the writings of Philip Melanchthon, the word *Predigtamt* always referred to the public office of the ministry. The same can be said for the vast majority of Luther's use of the term.[17] To be sure, this office is not to be understood clerically (as if the text were referring to a separate estate or walk of life [*Stand*]), and in an emergency, any Christian can fulfill this office, but, in fact, Article 5 refers specifically to clerics, that is, to those publicly called to teach and preach the gospel. Moreover, in an official document of this kind, to use the term *Predigtamt* meant the public office that included pastors, preachers, and bishops.

Furthermore, the Latin term used in Article 5, *ministerium*, also almost always referred to the same public office in the sixteenth century, especially when connected to teaching and administering the sacraments. There we read (Article 5.1 [Latin]): "So that we may obtain this faith, the ministry of teaching the gospel and administering the sacraments was instituted." The pervasive designation by the reformers of this office with the Latin word *ministerium* is itself noteworthy. Although the standard Latin dictionary, Lewis and Short, defines the use of the term *minister* in the Vulgate (Romans 15:16, 2 Corinthians 6:4, and Ephesians 3:7, 6:21) and ecclesiastical Latin as a "preacher of Christ" or "minister of religion," the editors themselves have actually confused later use of the English word, derived from Reformation recovery of the original meaning of the Latin term, with patristic usage. In his Latin translation of the Bible, Jerome rendered both *leitourgos* ("public servant") in Romans and *diakonos* ("servant/slave") in Ephesians and 2 Corinthians with the Latin *minister*, quite in line with the most basic meaning of that Latin term: "attendant, waiter, servant." Similarly, the Reformation often avoided using late-medieval terms like *priest, cleric,* or *spirituals* in favor of the simple word *minister,* and it designated the "Office of Preaching" as *ministerium,* a word that Jerome used in translating the Greek *diakonia* in Acts 6:4 and 2 Corinthians 6:3 and *leitourgia* in Hebrews 8:6. The servant quality of this office most profoundly shaped Reformation understanding.

The German is even more unambiguous: *Das Predigtamt* can only mean "the office of preaching," as the new English translation renders it.[18] This was always a public office and, in the neutral use of the term, "clerical." Indeed, Tappert's footnote and the one in the BSLK were intended to give space to the so-called *allgemeine Priestertum aller Gläubigen,* a phrase first associated with Luther's theology in the eighteenth or nineteenth century and much more at home in Pietism's platform of church reform, Philipp Jakob Spener's *Pia desideria,* and nowhere to be found in *The Book of Concord.* As we saw in chapter 1, it is with Spener that the spiritual priesthood of *all* the baptized received its decidedly political cast as the priesthood of the laity and resulted in the separation of the laity from the clergy—the very thing Luther's arguments against Roman clericalism were intended to overcome.[19] The only difference between late-medieval clericalism and Lutheran Pietism was that under Pietism the laity finally gained ascendancy over the clergy rather than the other way around. Either way, Luther's point is lost to church politics.

Thus, to begin any understanding of the public office of ministry (including both pastors and bishops) in the Lutheran confessions, one must begin where the Augsburg Confession itself does, with the office of preaching, *das Predigtamt,* in Article 5. There we discover several crucial aspects to any understanding of this public office. First, Melanchthon clearly linked the preaching office to justification itself: "To obtain such faith" (German) and "So that we may obtain this faith" (Latin). The alternative would be to imagine that the *gratis* or *aus Gnaden* ("freely" or "by grace") in Article 4 is simply pretend. That would be to define faith itself as a work (or, nowadays, a "decision") that we manufacture in order to set into motion the elaborate mechanism of obtaining Christ's grace. But Melanchthon knew better and actually reordered the Schwabach Articles to make the connection clearer.[20] The Holy Spirit produces faith through the means of gospel and sacraments.

Some interpreters have been fooled at this point by the speed with which Melanchthon moved from the "office" to the means of grace. Article 5 (German) reads, "God instituted the office of preaching, giving the gospel and the sacraments"—that is, the article seems to ignore the officeholders altogether. However, rather than construe this as a minimization of the public office of ministry, the language actually points to a radical reordering of the office. The (ministerial) office is transparent. It has to do with the actual delivery of the goods, the actual service to the gospel and the gospel's sacraments.[21] To call attention at this point in the Augsburg Confession's argument to the office per se would be to undermine the connection to justification by faith alone and destroy the very public office this article sets out to define.

Once the intrinsic transparency of the office becomes clear—that its point has to do with giving and, hence, serving (*ministerium*)—then the God-given nature of the office becomes even more revolutionary! The Latin's passive ("the ministry . . . was instituted"), which masks the subject of the verb, receives in the German its true origins: with God. "God instituted the office of preaching." Thus, authorization for the public office comes directly from God.[22] Just as faith can have no origin outside of God's Holy Spirit using the gospel and Sacraments, so the authority of the public office that delivers the Word (spoken and visible) comes from God alone.

The popularity, especially but not exclusively among nineteenth-century Americans, of the *Übertragungslehre*, a theory of transference, which argued that the so-called common priesthood of all believers transferred its authority to the public office of ministry, has no place in the interpretation of this article.[23] First, this theory developed in tandem with the increasing certainty that faith, too, arose from human exertion. (Similarly, one could argue that the notion that apostolically successful bishops can guarantee the purity of church doctrine grew up alongside the same synergistic impulses.) Second, any approach to the *Predigtamt* that derives its authority from human powers (congregational, presbyteral, episcopal, or individual) falls under Article 5's condemnation of those "who teach that we obtain the Holy Spirit without the external word of the gospel through our own preparation, thoughts, and works." Preparations, thoughts, and works may include assertions about congregational autonomy, episcopal apostolicity, or individual anointing. Third, to be sure, *authorization* to exercise the office involves the community and those to whom oversight has been entrusted. This is the point of Article 14. However, the authority exercised within the office, to proclaim the gospel and administer sacraments, comes from God alone. In sum, the article of justification by grace through faith on account of Christ alone demands the public office of preaching and administering the sacraments—a ministry that God institutes and empowers by the Holy Spirit and to which bishops and pastors (among others) belong.[24]

The other statements in Article 5 simply underscore the connection between this article and justification. Faith is a gift worked in us by the Holy Spirit through means (Article 5.2). The content of the gospel and sacraments is the message of justification by faith alone (Article 5.3). The Holy Spirit comes through the means God provides and neither through human effort (Article 5.4) nor outside of the means of grace. In sum, the article of justification by grace through faith on account of Christ alone demands the public office of preaching and administering the sacraments—an office that God institutes and empowers by the Holy Spirit and that is defined by service. It is all about the end.

The Text and Meaning of Article 14

Only in this (eschatological) context can a reader understand the brevity and complexity of Article 14, one of the most hotly contested articles among American Lutherans. The Latin version for Article 14 of the Augsburg Confession states: "Concerning church order [our churches] teach that no one should teach publicly in the church or administer the sacraments unless properly called [*rite vocatus*]."[25] With this, the shortest of the articles in the Confession, Philip Melanchthon says everything about church order so clearly and succinctly that subsequent readers often misunderstand his intentions completely.[26] The German version offers only a modicum of assistance: "Concerning church government it is taught that no one should publicly teach, preach, or administer the sacraments without a proper call."[27]

Historical and textual analysis provides some clarity. First, although titles for the first twenty-one articles were not part of the original document (they were first added to editions published in the seventeenth century), here they match the first words in this article. These words ("concerning church government" and "concerning church order") tell us specifically what this article addresses: how to order the public ministry of the church.

Second, the position of this article is also important. Melanchthon organized the Augsburg Confession (and other doctrinal statements) quite consciously. He began with the Word (Articles 1–6) and moved to the sacraments (Articles 9–13), placing the church (the marks of which are the Word and the sacraments) in between (Articles 7 and 8). In Article 15, he explained a reference to church practices made earlier in Article 7.3. So Article 14 stands on the border, so to speak, between the sacraments and the church. No wonder that in the Apology (13.11), Melanchthon suggested that one could understand ordination, interpreted now as referring to the public ministry of the Word (audible and visible), as a sacrament![28] Thus, Article 14 stands where it does—right next to the sacraments (Articles 9–13) and associated with the church

(Articles 7 and 8)—because those opposed to the evangelical party at Augsburg did not link ordination to the proclamation of God's word. Instead, they viewed it as a "sacrificial office," where priests offered to God on behalf of the people "unbloody" sacrifices for the forgiveness of sins.[29] Against this distortion, Article 14 argues that the public office can never contradict the heart of the good news itself (Article 4) or the delivery of that news through the public office of ministry (Article 5).

Third, one very important word in Article 14 is *public.* This is the eschatological purpose of church government and order: to see to it that what has been whispered in secret is shouted from the rooftops (Matthew 10:27). This emphasis contrasted directly to self-appointed, so-called radical preachers, who based their authority solely on themselves and their personal calls. Although the Roman authorities often accused Luther and the evangelicals of such usurpation of authority, in fact all the leaders of the evangelical movement were duly called pastors and preachers of the existing church. "The call," Luther once said at table, "hurts the devil very much."[30]

A fourth thing to note here is Melanchthon's inclusion of the verb "to teach." Philip Melanchthon himself was neither a pastor nor a preacher (two distinct offices in the churches of the late Middle Ages and Reformation). He was not ordained. Yet the largely mythical view of him as a "lay theologian" is completely anachronistic.[31] He was called as a teacher at the University of Wittenberg, first in 1518 as a member of the arts faculty and teacher of Greek, again in 1519 as a lecturer on the Bible in the theological faculty, and finally after 1526 as a professor in both faculties. In 1524, he became the first married rector of a European university. In this way, Melanchthon's position also fell under this article. Article 14 applies as fully to teachers as to those who preach and preside in congregations.

Thus, Article 14 describes the three central offices in the churches of the Reformation: teacher, preacher, and pastor. However, this does not mean that the confessional writers had what some have called a "functional" view of the ministry any more than they held an "ontological" view. In fact, as detailed in chapters 1 and 2, these two extremes do not describe Luther's theology of ministry at all, but instead, express ideas more at home either in Pietism or in late-medieval theology. The reformers consistently linked the public call with certain offices—offices established by Christ, mirrored in the Old Testament, and fostered in the ancient and early medieval church. Thus, "pastor" and "bishop" (the terms are interchangeable in the usage of the New Testament, the ancient church, and the Reformation) find their origins in the New Testament and ancient church. "Preacher" hearkens back to Peter in Acts 2 and to the Hebrew prophets— anyone who publicly bears a direct word of God to the people. In the Reformation churches, it was an office distinct from that of pastor. Teachers find a place in the lists of Ephesians 4:11 and 1 Corinthians 12:28, and in the Middle Ages, they became associated with the four great Latin fathers: Augustine, Jerome, Ambrose, and Gregory the Great.[32] The reformers are saying not that "anyone can be a pastor" but that "whoever does such things fulfills the very public office authorized by Christ and demanded by the Word."

In short, wherever the church "goes public" with the gospel, one finds the public office of ministry. Those who exercise such offices do so not because the "laity" or the "priesthood of all believers" understood politically bestows authority on the office, but because Christ vests the office with his authority through the Word that puts to death and makes alive. The authority of the office, then, is not held, but rather happens when this Word is spoken, water is poured, or bread is distributed. This explains why Article 5 (German) defines the "office of preaching" long before raising the question of church order. In fact, *how* a person enters the office is far less important than the fact *that* the office publicly bears the Word and the sacraments to the world under direct authority from Christ.

Article 14: Putting the Article in Its Place

As we have seen, much ink has been spilled over this article—a witness to the twentieth-century debt to pious nineteenth-century disputes. The Latin's *rite vocatus* has to do only with calling in a "regular manner," as the words *Kirchenregiment* and *ordo ecclesiastica* imply, and not with ritual and, hence, not with the necessity of using bishops in communion with the Roman papacy.[33] However, the terms *proper call* (German) and *properly* (Latin) *do* imply oversight. This intention becomes clear in developments throughout the 1530s and 1540s and is expressly stated in Melanchthon's 1540 additions to the Augsburg Confession.[34]

In 1534, as part of the negotiations with Henry VIII, Melanchthon was forced to defend the positive statements about the office of bishop found in documents written for negotiations with the French but that were based on the Augsburg Confession and the Apology. In a letter to the English ambassador Christopher Mont, which comes to us only in a sixteenth-century English translation, Melanchthon stated:

> When I name the ecclesiasticall power, I mean nott principally the primacye of the bishop of Rome, butt I spek generally of the authorite of bisshopps and chiefly I mean this discipline, by cause there bee certain bisshoppes the which oweth to ordre prists, the which shulde exercise the ecclesiasticall jugements and consider the doctrine. This accustomyd forme I wolde gladly have contynuyd in every nation, for of truthe it is necessarye that ther shuld bee certain as superintendents of whom the prists may be ordryd.[35]

After rejecting the notion that ordination be abolished or that it be performed by laypersons or other private persons, he continued:

> Paulus commawndyd Titus to ordre prists, and to Timothe he sayth: "Putt thy hands upon no man hastely," and therefore he willyd as

well the examination as power to ordre to be in the bisshoppes. He willid nott prists to bee ordryd withowte examination, and this examination he hath committyd to the bisshoppes to whom it apperteynth to holde stedfastly the doctrine of Christe. And therfor this hath byn observyd ever sens the begynnyng in the churche, that the bisshoppes shulde both: judge of them that shuld be ordred and also ordre them. . . . nother I see any cause wherfor it shuld bee lawfull to chawnge this custome of the churche, if the bisshoppes will ordre good teachers, that is to say, if the bisshoppes bee nott enimyes to the gospel, if they murder nott the good teachers, and if they will nott commit the rule of the churche to corrupt teachers.

This means that the English church received encouragement from the Saxon church, specifically from Philip Melanchthon, author of the Augsburg Confession and its Apology, to give bishops (understood: who preach the gospel) the power to ordain. That some Lutherans object to fellowship with Anglicans or Episcopalians simply because their bishops do all the ordaining means, ironically, that they are rejecting a principle Melanchthon insisted upon in negotiations with the English crown. To be sure, this does not prove the necessity of episcopal ordination, only that it cannot be ipso facto excluded as a possibility.

Then, in 1545, Melanchthon wrote the "ordination certificate," as it was called, for the consecration by Luther of Georg, Prince of Anhalt, as coadjutor bishop of Merseburg.[36] The document outlined duties specific to the office of bishop, basing these duties on Paul's injunction to Titus (1:5: "I left you behind in Crete for this reason, so that you . . . should appoint elders in every town") and Jesus' command to Peter (Luke 22:32: "And you, when you turn back, confirm your brothers"). Thus, the newly ordained bishop "knows that he also has been enjoined by the apostolic voice for this function, that he may ordain priests for teaching and ruling the Churches and may inspect their teaching and behavior." Here Melanchthon highlighted the specific duties of bishop, oversight of other pastors through visitation and ordination, giving them both a Pauline and a Petrine basis for authority.

Under these circumstances, when he published a fuller version of the Augsburg Confession in 1540, Melanchthon used the same verse from Titus 1 to expand Article 14 (see below). Of course, the same episcopal construal of this article was already present *in nuce* in the Apology (14). There, too, Melanchthon insisted that the evangelicals had no qualms about episcopal oversight, as long as that oversight conformed to the gospel. If it did not, as we have already seen, the office would lose its very transparency, and the gospel of justification by faith alone would be under threat from "enemies of the gospel."

In the Apology 14.2, as we shall discover below, Melanchthon also blamed the Roman bishops for dividing the church.[37] If church order no longer serves "a good and useful purpose." but instead persecutes those who confess and preach the gospel, then (and only then) evangelicals have no choice but to reject such cruelty and its perpetrators. The Word and sacraments that mark the church (Apology 14.4) cannot fail those who believe nor separate them from that church. The alternative (destruction of the Word and butchery of those who teach the truth) cannot be church, let alone the true office of oversight. Because of this, however, we must look for a proper definition of such oversight not in Article 14 but in Article 28 (see chapter 4). At the same time, we must realize that readers of the Augsburg Confession, following Article 5, gave the word *gospel* the same meaning Melanchthon used there: the free forgiveness of sins in Christ given through Word and sacrament and received by faith alone. This eliminates the temptation to define gospel in terms of church order—a temptation to which many, on both the congregational and the episcopal sides of current debates, easily succumb.

Structuring the Office of Ministry
in the Lutheran Confessions

There are limited hints in the Lutheran Confessions as to how the reformers structured the public office of ministry. Later sources demonstrate that, even in Article 14, Melanchthon was thinking about the responsibility of oversight in the form of bishops and superintendents. In 1540, Melanchthon produced an expanded version of the Augsburg Confession known as the *Variata*. A generation later, this version came under suspicion because of the way some used it to defend a less-than-Lutheran view of Christ's presence in the Lord's Supper. However, many later Lutheran theologians, including Martin Chemnitz and David Chytraeus (two authors of the Formula of Concord), rightly viewed the rest of the document as an expansion and clarification of the original.[38] In Article 14 (*Variata*), Melanchthon added a single sentence to show that he assumed bishops would regulate the public office of ministry. To the phrase *rite vocatus*, Melanchthon added: "As also Paul commanded Titus [1:5] that he should set up elders [presbyters] in the towns."[39] As we have seen, he then used this very instruction of Paul to Titus in the ordination certificate for one of the first evangelical bishops in order to indicate that the bishop alone was to perform all ordinations within his diocese.

However, not only the *Variata*, but also a document much more contemporaneous with the original Augsburg Confession indicates the role bishops were to play in ordering church life. The Apology, published in 1531, also dealt with the role of bishops. The opponents to the evangelical party at Augsburg had accepted Article 14 in their *Confutation*, but with the caveat that "canonical ordination" be used. This, of course, undermined the intent of Article 14 by attempting to force evangelicals to obey bishops opposed to the gospel.[40] Yet Melanchthon used the Apology at this point not to reject the office of bishop, but rather to attack its abuse. The subtlety of his argument is sometimes lost on later readers.

First, Melanchthon noted that his opponents accepted this article of the Augsburg Confession provided that the phrase *rite vocatus* meant the use of canonical ordination, that is, ordination by a bishop in communion with the Roman pope. Melanchthon responded by reminding his readers of the consistent position of the Saxon party and their allies at Augsburg.[41] Repeatedly—in private negotiations, in the Confession and other public documents, and in a variety of committees set up in August 1530 to deal with the looming split—they had made their position clear: "Give us freedom to preach, teach, and practice the gospel, and we will honor episcopal authority in the church." While Melanchthon reiterated that position here, he also made it clear that episcopal authority was not part of the gospel and the authority bestowed by Christ on the public office. It was, rather, an arrangement "established by human authority."[42]

However, Melanchthon did not leave it at that. He also placed this human authority in direct line with Article 15 and the proper role of such human regulations in the church. Such canonical ordination "was instituted by the Fathers for a good and useful purpose." This he contrasted in Apology 14.2 with the behavior of bishops in his day, who either compelled priests to condemn and reject the teaching of the Augsburg Confession or, "by new and unheard cruelty," put them to death. The conclusion is crucial: "This prevents our priests from acknowledging such bishops." This "cruelty of the bishops" is the actual cause of the neglect of "canonical order," for which these bishops must answer to God. Thus, the heart of the matter for Melanchthon in the Apology was not existence of bishops or their exercise of authority to ordain, but rather what was at stake (again) was the gospel. He concluded with (eschatological) fervor: "Let the bishops ask themselves how they will give an answer to God for breaking up the church. We have clear consciences on this matter since we know that our confession is true, godly, and catholic."[43]

Further, Melanchthon viewed this dispute in terms of evangelical ecclesiology. The church exists among those "who rightly teach the Word of God and rightly administer the sacraments" (Apology 14.4). This definition, taken directly from Article 7, makes the church not an institution but an event. However, in this situation, this description of such a positive event implied for Melanchthon also its opposite, so he continued: "It does not exist among those who not only try to destroy the Word of God with their edicts, but who also butcher those who teach what is right and true." It is the destruction of the Word and its ministers that completely undermines the church-event, because without the word of God there can be no church. In our own day, popular, "success-oriented," "purpose-driven" groups have arisen (some of which, perhaps as a matter of truth in advertising, do not even call themselves churches), where the Bible is not read (or read only sparingly and then only to focus on moral teachings), the preaching is reduced to moral exhortations and the sacraments are completely neglected or celebrated as if nothing happened in Baptism and as if Christ were not present in the Supper. They are not church, according to Article 7 and Melanchthon's definition in Apology 14. However, they are also not so much destroying and persecuting true believers as ignoring them. Their assemblies are simply nonevents, not anti-events.

Finally, as we will discover in chapter 4, Article 28 provides a lengthy discussion of church order, which Melanchthon labeled in the German, "Concerning the Power of Bishops" and, in Latin, "Concerning the Church's Power." The mixing of ecclesiastical and secular power, a problem that dominates the early part of this article, has thankfully disappeared from the church.[44] The reformers were willing to put up with people who were both bishops, in the true sense of the term, and princes—as long as they carefully separated these two realms.[45] Melanchthon went to great lengths in this article to define the office of bishop, which is equivalent to the pastoral office. "Our people teach as follows. According to the gospel the power of the keys or of the bishops is a power and command of God to preach the gospel, to forgive or retain sin, and to administer and distribute the sacraments."[46]

He supported this with a reference to John 20:21-23. Further on in the article, he reiterated this position but added several other duties. "Consequently, according to divine right it is the office of the bishop to preach the gospel, to forgive sin, to judge doctrine and reject doctrine that is contrary to the gospel, to exclude from the Christian community the ungodly whose ungodly life is manifest—not with human power but with God's Word alone."[47] He insisted that, in line with Luke 10:16, parishioners and teachers owe obedience to such bishops, as long as what they teach accords with the gospel. As far as matters that fall outside the gospel—whether it is jurisdiction over marriage (par. 29) or church practices (par. 30)—everything depends on the gospel. "Bishops do not have the power to institute or establish something contrary to the gospel."[48] Human regulations simply serve the good order of the church, but they do not bring persons closer to God and the gospel. "For the chief article of the gospel must be maintained, that we obtain the grace of God through faith in Christ without our merit and do not earn it through service of God instituted by human beings."[49]

Other documents in *The Book of Concord* say much the same thing but also discuss ordination as a peculiar right of bishops. Luther wrote in the Smalcald Articles that "if the bishops wanted to be true bishops and to attend to the church and the gospel, then a person might—for the sake of love and unity but not out of necessity—give them leave to ordain and confirm us and our preachers."[50] In the Treatise on the Power and Primacy of the Pope, to which we will return in chapter 5, Melanchthon referred back to the discussion in the Augsburg Confession and its Apology and provided a brief discussion of ordination—a right granted *by human authority* to bishops and abrogated only "when the regular bishops become enemies of the gospel or are unwilling to ordain."[51] As with the right of midwives to baptize, only the eschatological urgency of proclaiming the gospel in the face of heresy or true tyranny would ever give Christians leave to ordain without permission from the one entrusted with oversight.[52]

The Public Office of Ministry
in the Twenty-First Century

It is the office of bishops, pastors, and other leaders in today's church to apply the witness of Scripture and the Lutheran Confessions to the problems the church faces. Here are a few suggestions for beginning such a discussion. Consider Philip Melanchthon's call as teacher and *mutatis mutandis*, that of other teachers in Lutheran seminaries—"lay" or ordained. Current concern over "lay" licensure has never touched upon whether laypersons should teach at Lutheran seminaries. Seminaries seek to provide the best teachers for future leaders in the church, who in thought, word, and deed show commitment to parish ministry. Questions about "lay" or "ordained" arise only secondarily and only in relation to the actual experience and commitments of individual teachers.

The question of "laypersons" (synodically approved ministers) presiding regularly at Holy Communion (where using the term *layperson* is itself an importation of medieval terminology into evangelical theology) might be resolved if the ordination and call of such persons were held not by the individual ordained as if they were rights but by the synod council and bishop. Then such people would be clearly set apart for the public office of ministry but not in such a way as to confuse their limited abilities and call with those of other ministers. Just as we do not confuse an EMT with an emergency room physician—and yet both have crucial offices to fulfill in a medical emergency—so, too, there can be a variety of public ministries serving the Word. The crucial thing is delivering the gospel.

Of course, one may ask why the bishop or synod council should hold such an ordination or call or how we would know how they even have such a right to do this. But underneath questions like these lurks a problem, or disease, in American culture itself, one that is so self-evident that we are nearly incapable of meeting it head-on: our addiction to individualism. That is to say that the images for church in Scripture and tradition (body, people, city) and the model for the public ministry (namely, service to gospel and church) are not simply foreign to but are directly opposed to our upbringing. Service to the gospel in the church, simply put, is countercultural.[53]

Then there is the actual relation between the office (however we may fill it) and the gospel. A church that ordains or otherwise sets people apart who preach works righteousness and undermine trust in God is guilty of the same contempt of the gospel for which the reformers criticized their opponents. Thus, pious-sounding preachers enraptured by one kind of social or personal action or another may be guilty of such deception. Ritually sensitive sacerdotes addicted either to growing mega-churches or to repristinating the liturgical past may slip into similar traps. Bishops, pastors, and teachers of the church hold offices of oversight in the church to see that such things do not happen and to preserve the eschatological edge of God's consoling gospel in Christ.

Yet, all of these matters simply touch on the periphery of the public office of ministry. If there is a crisis in this office for the church, that crisis is only indirectly reflected in such matters as who should ordain or who should be ordained. The real crisis rests in the sad fact that few people seem to know what a pastor is supposed to do: we have lost sight of the true end or goal of this office. We are willing to have "resident theologians" (that is, resident scholars or rabbis) or "givers of pastoral care" (that is, counselors and advisors) or CEOs (that is, crack administrators) or community organizers (that is, social workers) or friends, but who wants someone whose chief calling is to speak publicly for fifteen minutes a week and to preside at strange rituals of washing and eating? The jokes about pastors working only one hour a week—of which even the most evenly tempered among us get tired—may contain (unwittingly) more than a grain of truth. Those called to the public office of ministry have no more to say or do in our vocations than Mary Magdalene: "It's over, boys, he rose!" The end of the office of ministry (that is, its goal) is finally simply to announce the end—of the law, of our lives, of sin, of death, of the world—by announcing Christ's end: cross and resurrection. Paul's curious plea in Romans 10 ("How shall they hear without a preacher?") sums up everything a pastor, bishop, preacher, or teacher gets to do: rise to his or her feet and announce the end of the world in Christ by faith alone. In the end, the Word (aural and visible) makes all the difference and makes this curious, God-given office what it is: God's gift to the Christian assembly, the church.

CHAPTER 4

BISHOPS IN THE AUGSBURG CONFESSION: SERVANTS OF THE CRUCIFIED

In his peculiarly trenchant fashion, Heiko Oberman pleaded in his biography of Martin Luther that to understand Luther one must break historical sound barriers—that is, one must attempt to crawl out from under the typical prejudices of our times to appreciate the very different times in which Luther lived.[1] For Oberman, this meant recovering a new respect for Luther's understanding of the devil. In like manner, present debates over the office of ministry in the Lutheran church demand a similar high-speed journey into the past. We labor not only under modern misconceptions but also under the accretions of the past—debates of nineteenth-century scholars, which in turn rested upon the misinterpretations of their pious and rationalistic forebears. More recent demands of the ecumenical movement have, in many instances, simply deepened earlier divides and caught Luther and Melanchthon in the clutches of debates largely foreign to their own theology and experience. To appreciate fully the reformers' understanding of the evangelical episcopate is to enter a world where the questions of our day and age find few direct solutions.

As Oberman himself demonstrated in *Luther: Man between God and the Devil*, the result of breaking the historical sound barrier may allow Lutheranism's most cherished documents to echo anew through some of the most intractable ecumenical problems of our day. In this case, as we will discover in this and the following chapter through a close reading of three of the most important texts on this issue in *The Book of Concord* (the

Augsburg Confession, the Apology, and the Treatise on the Power and Primacy of the Pope), the reformers held a far more positive view of the evangelical office of bishop, derived from the public office of ministry, than has often been depicted in the secondary literature or contemporary debate. What matters is the authority of the gospel and the good order of the church. Moreover, certain sixteenth-century strictures against the papacy and bishops in communion with Rome must be understood more generally within the context of the Reformation rejection of tyranny over the gospel. This tyranny, as more than 450 years of history has taught us, can take not only episcopal but also presbyteral, congregational, or even individualistic forms.

What Scholars Are Saying about Bishops in Early Lutheranism

With notable exceptions, recent literature on Lutheran bishops has only occasionally broken Oberman's historical sound barrier. The following brief look at some of the material simply points out recurring problems without pretending to offer a complete review of all relevant literature.

Material written in English is often dependent on German scholarship and does not always provide helpful approaches to the historical material. For example, Merlyn E. Satrom, in "Bishops and Ordination in the Lutheran Reformation of Sixteenth-Century Germany," is almost exclusively dependent on secondary literature.[2] He does at least point out that bishops were not unheard of in the German (Lutheran) context of the sixteenth century. In his influential article "The Historic Episcopate and the Lutheran Confessions," Robert Goeser tries to summarize the position of early Lutherans leading up to the Augsburg Confession.[3] He mistakenly imagines that Luther only hesitatingly supported the Saxon compromise (obedience to Roman bishops in exchange for married priests, communion in both kinds, and an end to private, sacrificial masses), a premise based on the questionable work of

Wilhelm Maurer. He does not understand that the omission in the Visitation Articles of references to ordination by superintendents arose out of political impossibility. He imagines (p. 220) that the Torgau articles actually reject bishops *per se*, when in fact they contain the standard rejection of bishops who will not tolerate the gospel. The Saxon compromise did not imply church order without oversight, despite Goeser's assertions (p. 221). He even states, "The first part of the CA has really nothing to do with Article 28" (p. 222). Finally, Goeser asserts that Article 14 of the Augsburg Confession could not mean ordination by bishops.[4]

One particularly helpful contribution was made by Ralph F. Smith, the tragically deceased professor of liturgy at Wartburg Seminary in Dubuque, Iowa, in his *Luther, Ministry, and Ordination Rites in the Early Reformation Church*.[5] There, based on the work of Peter Brunner,[6] he describes in detail Luther's 1542 ordination of Nicholas von Amsdorf as bishop of Naumburg. Unfortunately, he misunderstands Luther's position when he says, "By interpreting episcopal consecrating as ordination Luther indirectly pleaded the case he had made at other times that the presbyterate and episcopate were identical" (p. 158). (In fact, von Amsdorf had already been ordained a priest.) The identity only stretches as far as the overarching office of public ministry (by divine right: *de iure divino*) of Word and sacrament. However, by human right (*de iure humano*), the two were different, since the one always included oversight. He partially corrects himself by arguing for one office of the *ministerium* and different "roles" (p. 161).[7]

On the German scene, the literature is also mixed. The article "Das evangelische Bischofsamt," by Gerhard Tröger in the *Theologische Realenzyklopädie*, the premier German theological reference work, contains two historical oversights.[8] First, Tröger does not take seriously that, especially in Germany, the term *Bischof* had other connotations and, thus, that to understand the evangelical office of bishop, one needs to take very seriously the reformers' translation (using principles of dynamic equivalency) into Latin: *Superintendentes*. Moreover, the title of *summus episcopus* for the prince of a territory, which to my knowledge is never used by Luther nor Melanchthon, was equally a political categorization having much more to do with strains after the Peace of Augsburg of 1555 than anything else. As we shall see below in the discussion of Article 28 of the Augsburg Confession, the phrase *de iure humano* [by human right] is not necessarily a diminution of the episcopal office, but rather makes clear that some of its authority falls under Romans 13, while (*de iure divino* [by divine right]) other parts fall under John 20 (or Matthew 16 and 18). Tröger does underscore the centrality of visitation and oversight. The issue of succession, which he also discusses, is generally relevant only to modern discussions of authority in the church.

Perhaps the most telling comment in the work of Hans-Otto Wölber is the first sentence: "Without a doubt, there exists a huge uncertainty concerning the essence and form of a Lutheran office of bishop."[9] Like many other German commentators, Wölber's analysis suffers under the modern challenge of "Staatskirchentum" ("state church-ness," quoting Jakob Burckhardt). Because he does not take into account the historical context or the rhetorical structure of Article 28 (see below), Wölber bemoans the fact that that article does not mention either ordination (not yet practiced among evangelicals) or visitation (the actual matter of dispute in Augsburg). Although he does touch upon the heart of the Augsburg Confession's radical proposal—the divine authority of the bishop is a matter of administering the word of God— he mixes the two kingdoms (law and gospel) in his discussion of the third use of the law because he does not realize that for Melanchthon episcopal authority arises by human right, that is, under the first use of the law.[10]

Bernhard Lohse, in "The Development of the Offices of Leadership in the German Lutheran Churches: 1517–1918," in *Episcopacy in the Lutheran Church?*, makes a mistake in his first sentence: "Luther did not outline any definite program for the implementation of the implications of the Reformation nor did he make any specific proposals for a new evangelical Church organization."[11] This contradicts Luther's work on the German Mass (*Deutsche Messe*) and the Instruction by the Visitors (*Unterricht der Visitatoren*) in the 1520s and any of the countless other memoranda of the 1530s and 1540s. Lohse's assumption (p. 52) that Luther rejected episcopal claims of the right to rule in the church is incorrect, as proven by Luther's attempts to establish an episcopal leadership of the church (also p. 52). When Lohse states that there is "really no fundamental difference between the bishop and pastor," it is too general a statement to be of much help. His dismissal of the work of Helmut Lieberg is without adequate foundation.[12] Equating bishop and pastor (*Pfarrherr*) is not the same as equating bishop and preacher (*Prediger*) or teacher (*Lehrer*). For these reasons (and others), his exposition of Article 28 (pp. 57–58) underestimates the positive assessment of bishops by the reformers. His comments about differences between Luther and Melanchthon on the role of princes in church government have been corrected by James Estes.[13]

The most helpful collection of essays, edited by Luther's famous biographer Martin Brecht, is *Martin Luther und das Bischofsamt*.[14] Here one discovers the kind of historical work necessary for further reflection on the question of bishops in the Lutheran confessions. Brecht's own "The Exegetical Foundation of the Office of Bishop" (pp. 10–14) points out the centrality of Titus 1:5 already in Luther's reflections in the Leipzig Debates and in his tract *Address to the Christian Nobility*. Thus, Brecht writes: "[Luther] consciously argued here using the New Testament material, to which the highest revelatory authority is given. Titus 1:5-7 is taken as a divine statute showing that in each city there should be at least one bishop or more. The one office (of bishops and priests) is reckoned as having been established on the basis of divine law. It is not derived from the priesthood of all believers" (p. 11).[15]

Heinz-Meinolf Stamm argues both for the continuity of Luther's thought and his reliance on Jerome for the singular public office of the ministry and his criticism not of episcopal power but of any claim (by divine right) for the papacy.[16] Gottfried Krodel uses Luther's tract from 1522 to show how Luther envisioned an evangelical office of bishop (later realized to a great degree in Samland and Pomesania).[17] He points out how important it is to distinguish Luther's various uses of the word *bishop* (either as an expression of those in communion with Rome or as an overseer in the church for the sake of the gospel).

In a clever reflection on the situation in Leisnig in 1522, Martin Brecht[18] argues that, even in the tract that permits congregations to call pastors against the will of the bishops in league with Rome, "Luther tries much more to prove that the bishop and congregation normally must work together in the call process" (p. 67).[19] (This would mean not only that when a bishop goes bad, a congregation must act alone, but also that when a congregation betrays the gospel, the bishop must intervene.) Ken Miura and Martin Brecht's analysis of Luther's 1523 tract on ministry (*On the Instituted Ministries*) points out the similarities between it and *That a Christian Assembly or Congregation Has the Right and Authority to Judge All Teaching*.[20] However, as important as the role of the community is, the authors also point out that "more clearly than in that instance the episcopal/pastoral character of the leading urban church office is nevertheless recognizable."

Markus Wriedt looks at Luther's use of the title "bishop" in his letters and discovers (after appropriately limiting his conclusions) that Luther used the title for those who are city pastors.[21] The office to which these titles refer involves especially oversight over congregations' administration and organization (particularly the institution of evangelical worship) but also questions of managing personnel, solving theological disputes, and representing the church to the larger world. All of these things fall under his favorite title for such pastors, namely, *servus* or *minister Dei, Christi,* or *ecclesiae*. Despite his kind attempts to rescue Lohse's thesis (cited above), Wriedt actually insists that Luther's behavior "gives support for the supposition that according to Luther's understanding, the church should be structured in an episcopal manner." Despite comments about synodical structures (p. 92), "for Luther a church without a bishop is finally unthinkable."

Brecht's remarks about church visitations are less satisfying.[22] He does not fully take seriously the historical situation and the difficulty of using a word like *bishop* to describe the work of visitation. The visitation was a direct challenge to the actual bishops of Luther's day and, therefore, could not mean a return to an episcopal system in the narrow (papal) sense of the term. James Schaaf sheds more light on the problem by indicating that Luther understood the bishop's office to be one of oversight over preaching, celebrating of the sacraments, and teaching.[23] Whatever else the Christian prince as "Emergency bishop" was, he could not preach, but rather could only see to it that others did.

In Rolf Decot's article, we have an excellent analysis of Luther's tract *Admonition to the Clergy*.[24] Luther, like Melanchthon, strictly followed the electoral Saxon compromise and would allow the (Roman) bishops if they would give the evangelicals the right to preach the gospel. Decot (p. 116) sees in this writing several basic convictions of Luther: that bishops are without question a part of the evangelical church order, that the bishops of the old church held legitimate offices but just did not exercise them properly, that the main function of a bishop is the proclamation of the gospel, and that other functions are simply not listed here (as they are, pace Brecht, in the *Unterricht der Visitatoren*).

Brecht's remarks about ordination rightly point out that Luther's Smalcald Articles accepts ordination by bishops.[25] Finally, Irmgard Höß and Hans-Ulrich Delius describe three cases where Wittenberg's theologians endorsed (or, in the case of Kammin, denied) evangelical bishops.[26] Only in the case of Georg von Anhalt in Merseburg could one argue for a model of evangelical episcopacy, especially since the political and ecclesiastical mixture in the other two instances did little to enhance the gospel. Although, in the case of Naumburg, Luther could write that the Roman bishop (Julius Pflug) and his supportive cathedral canons were already deposed by virtue of their breaking the first table of the law (and thus the installation of another bishop did not constitute oath breaking), von Amsdorf was caught in the political designs of the elector whose defeat at the hands of the emperor ended the "experiment."

Article 28: The Evangelical Office of Oversight

One place to turn to gain new clarity about the office of bishop is Article 28 of the Augsburg Confession.[27] Failure to appreciate the rhetorical shape of Melanchthon's arguments here has prevented readers from getting the most out of this article. To begin with, we must realize that Article 28 rests squarely on Articles 1–21, the doctrinal articles. If the first twenty-one articles were shown not to be catholic, then the evangelicals in Augsburg would have had no choice but to obey bishops in communion with Rome.[28] Melanchthon designed Article 28 to tie the office of bishop to teaching the gospel and rightly administering the sacraments (Articles 1–21, especially 5) and to demonstrate that the evangelical party's refusal to obey bishops who subvert the gospel and sacraments did not constitute a breach in the catholic faith. In so doing, Melanchthon delimited (but did not eliminate) episcopal authority in two ways: first by invoking the distinction between the two kingdoms (pars. 1–29) and then by defining the purpose of human ordinances in the church (pars. 30–75).

In most interpretations of the Augsburg Confession, even the best commentators have overlooked Melanchthon's skills in constructing this article according to rhetorical principles outlined in his 1531 edition of his textbook on rhetoric. In not only the Apology but also in the Confession, Melanchthon's careful use of rhetoric shines through, especially in Articles 20 and 28.[29] By taking this rhetorical tour de force into account, we will understand more clearly how he built his argument and what his overall point was.[30] This, in turn, will lead to more clarity about the role of bishops in the early evangelical movement.

THE RHETORICAL FORM OF ARTICLE 28

In his handbook on rhetoric from 1531, Melanchthon insisted that ecclesial debates over theological principles best employed the Ciceronian *genus iudiciale*, a type of speech used in a court of law, especially by a defense lawyer. Melanchthon modeled his comments in Article 28 on such a genre. Such a speech begins with an *exordium* (although this is optional), moves to the *narratio*, which gives the history of the case and includes the *status controversiae*, or main issue of contention, then explicates the *confirmatio*, which provides the main arguments in favor of the speaker's position. After this, the speaker or writer then provides a *confutatio* (that is, a section that overturns, or confutes, an opponent's arguments), and ends with a *peroratio*, which concludes the speech either with either a summary of the main points or an emotional appeal.

Exordium and *Narratio* (1–4; *BC 2000*, 90–93). In constructing Article 28, Melanchthon followed this rhetorical scheme quite closely, with one surprising twist in the middle of the article, where an accusation (reproof, or *objurgatio*) comes precisely where one would expect the *confutatio* to begin.[31] How does this work? As Melanchthon himself admits, the *genus iudiciale* does not necessarily need an *exordium* when used in theological debate.[32] Thus, paragraphs 1–4 function only loosely as an introduction, but do outline the *status controversiae* for the entire article. Indeed, Melanchthon constructed this opening section more as the first part of the *narratio* in order to introduce both issues (two kingdoms and authorization of human ordinances in the church), with the relation between the two carefully spelled out. By using (in par. 2) a standard "not only . . . but also" (*non solum . . . sed etiam*) construction, Melanchthon showed that the mixture of the two kingdoms ("the power of bishops with the secular sword") led to two kinds of abuses: new forms of worship (*Gottesdienst* or *cultus*), with their attendant burdening of consciences *and* the deposition of emperors and kings.[33] Precisely because his opponents claimed that the right to possess the second authority (to depose rulers) rested upon the first (to establish new forms of worship), Melanchthon placed his discussion of the second issue, framed as a rhetorically charged attack on the misuse of proper episcopal authority in establishing new forms of worship, in the *confutatio*.

In the *narratio*, some of Melanchthon's comments, grounded in the distinction of the two kingdoms, echoed the kind of late-medieval conciliarism still likely to find a hearing among many at the imperial diet. "Such outrage has long since been condemned by learned and devout people in Christendom" (Article 28.3). But he also appealed to another deeply held belief: that there should not be a confusion of callings (*"aus diesem unordentlichen Gemenge"* or *"ex hac confusione maxima"*).[34] This allowed him to make this first issue one of definition—stock-in-trade for Melanchthon, who later used it in constructing the arguments of the Apology, Article 4.

The apparently widespread condemnation of this mixing by many in the church (the critical edition of the Lutheran Confessions gives no specific references at this point) sets up the chief argument of this article, which is the heart of the *narratio*. Because so many "learned and devout people" have condemned this, "our people have been compelled, in order to comfort consciences, to indicate the difference between spiritual and secular power, sword, and authority. They have taught that, because of God's command, everyone should honor and esteem with all reverence both authorities and powers as the two highest gifts of God on earth" (Article 28.4). Crucial here is the reference to the comfort of consciences. This provides a link between the distinction of the two governments (which are God's gifts) and the gospel of justification by faith alone, which always serves to comfort terrified consciences.[35] From this comfort flow a proper honor and esteem for both authorities.

Confirmatio (5–29; *BC 2000*, 92–95). The heart of the *confirmatio*, which outlines the evangelical argument in the dispute, follows in paragraphs 5–29. In this case, to remedy *"das unordentliche Gemenge"* (the disordered mixture) Melanchthon resorted to his favorite cure: proper definition.[36] Paragraphs 5–7 defined what the power of the bishops is using language that echoed Article 5 and concluding with two proof texts (John 20:21-23 and Mark 16:15 [Latin only]).[37] Paragraphs 8–10 defined the exercise of this power—a typically Melanchthonian move.[38] In this case, Melanchthon noted that the number of people among whom this authority is exercised is unimportant and is simply a function of one's calling (*Beruf*). Moreover, and this will set up the contrast to secular authority, the "*ministerium verbi et sacramentorum*" (ministry of Word and sacraments) handles "eternal things and benefits."[39] Again, true to the *loci* method that undergirded his thought, Melanchthon provided several proof texts (Romans 1:16 and Psalm 119:50 [Latin only]). Melanchthon concluded (par. 10) that such an office did not interfere with that of magistrates, which he proceeded to define (par. 11).

Here Melanchthon solved a problem that would bedevil later generations. He expressly refused to follow the destructive definition of bishops that placed them over other pastors. Yet it is not that he denied power to bishops, but that, in an attempt to return to the definition of bishop used in the early church, he recognized that head pastors in a city or town (*Pfarrherren*) exercise the same level of spiritual authority as any bishop. For Melanchthon, the problem was not so much who ordains or how many parishes or congregants one controls but whether one deals in eternal or temporal things.

Having provided these (proper) definitions, Melanchthon then offered the conclusion to his logical argument (pars. 12–13), introduced appropriately with "therefore" *darumb* (Latin: *igitur*). The spiritual Governance should not invade an office alien to it. Melanchthon supported this purity of purpose (pars. 14–17) with a host of biblical texts (John 18:36, Luke 12:14, Philippians 3:20, and 2 Corinthians 10:4), the first two of which were also cited in the so-called Torgau articles.

With this, Melanchthon brought the heart of his *confirmatio* to a close, using language reminiscent of the preceding (par.

18): "In this way our people distinguish the offices of the two authorities and powers and direct that both be honored as the highest gifts of God on earth." Only here, and constructed as a clever aside, did Melanchthon mention (par. 19) what for the Holy Roman Empire was an obvious exception: its bishops were also princes of the empire. "That has nothing at all to do with the office of the gospel." It comprises a completely different set of tasks to be performed (Latin, *alia functio*).

This statement, when put into the form of a question, is perhaps the most lasting contribution Melanchthon's argument may make to our present conversations. What has this or that to do "with the office of the gospel"? In the face of this question, the power grabs of clergy or laity, the anti-institutional dreams of some in the New World and elsewhere, and the romantic dreams of medieval bishoprics in modern dress must give way. Even our ecumenical schemes, when they lose sight of the gospel, will find evangelical reorientation under this sign: what has this or that to do "with the office of the gospel"?

What follows in paragraphs 20–29 is the part of the *confirmatio* consisting in a collection of proofs for Melanchthon's central claim, in this case adduced as a corollary to his definitions—that is, since bishops do have authority over the gospel, Melanchthon had to define the nature (and limits) of obedience accorded to them. He began in the Latin version with a repetition of the *status*: "So [*igitur*], when asking about the jurisdiction of bishops, one must distinguish political rule [*imperium*] from the church's jurisdiction [*ecclesiastica iurisdictio*]." What followed, especially in the Latin, must have greatly surprised the English court (see chapter 3), to say nothing of others who wished to rid the church of episcopal power (such as was the case in the city of Nuremberg, which still signed the Augsburg Confession). He wrote:

> Consequently, according to the gospel, or, as they say, by divine right, this jurisdiction belongs to the bishops as bishops (that is, to those to whom the ministry of Word and sacraments has been committed): to

forgive sins, to reject teaching that opposes the gospel, and to exclude from the communion of the church the ungodly whose ungodliness is known—doing all this not with human power but by the Word. *In this regard, churches are bound by divine right to be obedient to the bishops, according to the saying* [Luke 10:16], *"Whoever listens to you listens to me."*[40]

Thus, Melanchthon focused the bishop's office on the teaching office and the office of the keys (narrowly construed). Bishops are defined in the spirit and with the words of Article 5: "those to whom the ministry of Word and sacraments has been committed." Bishops are servants of the Word and sacraments. Then, using a favorite proof text of his opponents, Melanchthon insisted that bishops must be obeyed.[41] However, he immediately followed this concession with the single caveat that was, in fact, the heart of the dispute. Since episcopal authority comes from the gospel, bishops lose their authority "whenever they teach, institute, or introduce something contrary to the gospel." Melanchthon proved this by heaping up authorities (a rhetorical *congeries*), including biblical citations (Matthew 7:15, Galatians 1:8, 2 Corinthians 13:8, 10), canon law, and Augustine. Again, given the political realities of the empire, Melanchthon noted (par. 29) that bishops might also exercise civil authority (especially in marital law) and insisted that princes are to step in "whether they like it or not" when bishops fail to do their duty.

Confutatio/Objurgatio (30–75; *BC 2000*, 94–103). At this juncture, Melanchthon introduced the second question into the dispute, but with such a change in rhetoric as to constitute a different kind of argument (and a different part of the speech). To be sure, the question itself flows directly from the preceding. If one cannot follow bishops when they directly contradict the gospel, can they be followed in matters of church ceremonies and regulations at all? Melanchthon shifted the argument from an external one (episcopal power over against political power) to an internal one (episcopal power in the church). However, the question also expressed the opponents' objections. Bishops, notably the pope, could intervene in political matters precisely because they had supreme authority over the church itself, where no prince dared to intrude.[42]

The way Melanchthon introduced the question indicated to the reader an important shift in argumentation and recalled the opening paragraphs of the entire article. Having used the word *disputationes* to introduce the entire article (par. 1), he now reintroduced the verbal form of the term with an appropriate prepositional phrase (par. 30: "*Praeter haec disputatur*"; German: "*Weiter disputiert man auch*" [further, one also disputes]).[43] Moreover, as mentioned above, the actual dispute was foreshadowed in his comments in paragraph 2. Indeed, he was introducing an argument not found in the Torgau articles but one that was in fact one of the charges of heresy published by John Eck just prior to the convening of the imperial diet.[44] However, it was not simply a completely separate topic, but a part of the overall rhetorical structure. It comes exactly where one would expect Melanchthon to deal with objections from the opponents.

What would remind the reader of a proper *confutatio* is the way Melanchthon summarized (for the first time in this article) the arguments of the opposition (pars. 31–33).[45] They cited John 16:12-13, Acts 15:20, 29, and the changing of the Sabbath from Saturday to Sunday, contrary to the Ten Commandments.[46] He then refuted these arguments at length (pars. 34–75), dealing specifically with the change in the Sabbath (pars. 53–68). His concluding remarks (pars. 69–75) succinctly summarized the Saxon negotiating position used throughout the diet and expressed Melanchthon's own conversations with Cardinal Campeggio.[47]

According to the rules of rhetoric, in a *confutatio,* Melanchthon did not have to prove his opponents totally wrong; he only had to point out obvious cases where bishops in fact did not have authority: namely (based on the definition of the office above) to institute something contrary to the gospel. He chose two objections. Bishops decreed that certain worship (not evil in itself) could merit satisfaction for sin (pars. 35–38), and they made the breaking of such human traditions a sin (pars. 39–40). Here Melanchthon managed to move the discussion back to the heart of Articles 1–21: justification by grace through faith on account of Christ alone (Articles 4–6 and Article 20) and the distinction between law and gospel (Articles 5, 12, 15, and 20).

What makes this section a reproof (or *objurgatio*) rather than a simple *confutatio* (refutation) is its style. Not only did Melanchthon shift the argument to the heart of the gospel, he also increased the rhetorical heat, so to speak. Unlike the arguments in the first half of this article, the reader suddenly encountered phrases like, "Now it is *patently* contrary to God's command and Word," and, "[bishops] *burden Christendom* with bondage to the law" (*Knechtschaft des Gesetzes*). Some bishops had even been deceived by the example of the Law of Moses and had confused breaking human ordinances for mortal sin, of which confusion Melanchthon provided five examples.[48]

To express his outrage, Melanchthon turned up the rhetoric: "Where did bishops get the right to impose such traditions on the churches in order to ensnare consciences?"[49] Such behavior ran squarely against the council of both Peter (Acts 15:10) and Paul (2 Corinthians 10:8), the patron saints of the bishop of Rome. "Why do they increase sins through such traditions?" With the code words "ensnare consciences" and "increase sins," Melanchthon struck a blow for the heart of Reformation theology: true freedom in the gospel. In contrast to all this (introduced with "*doch*" and "*verum*"), Melanchthon introduced *clara testimonia* (clear testimonies) of Scripture (pars. 43–48), beginning with a text on which he had written extensively elsewhere: Colossians 2:16, 2:20-23.[50] Again, because of the rhetorical nature of this confutation, he did not need to prove his case, but needed only to raise objections to his opponents' assumptions. He ended with a rhetorical flourish, posing what he considered three irrefutable questions: "If, then, bishops have the power to burden the churches with innumerable ordinances and to ensnare consciences, why does divine Scripture so frequently prohibit the making and keeping of human ordinances? Why does it call them teachings of the devil? Could the Holy Spirit possibly have warned against all this in vain?"[51]

Finally (in pars. 50–51), he concluded the entire section (introduced in the Latin text with *igitur* [therefore]) by linking the bishops' behavior to the gospel, or rather, to opposing the gospel (*dem Evangelio entgegen*). Under these conditions, bishops cannot compel such observation, since Christian freedom, as Paul taught in Galatians 5:1, must be preserved. "For the chief article of the gospel must be maintained, that we obtain the grace of God through faith in Christ without our merit and do not earn it through service of God [*Gottesdienst*] instituted by human beings" (par. 52).

Having dismissed this episcopal arrogance (that is, *not* serving the gospel), Melanchthon turned his attention to the specific proofs of his opponents: the decrees of the Council of Jerusalem (dealt with briefly in pars. 65–66) and the changing of the Sabbath from Saturday to Sunday. Because this constituted one of the charges in John Eck's *404 Articles*, Melanchthon had to devote more space (pars. 53–64) to it. He began with a basic distinction, which might be called an ecclesial first use of the law. Bishops and pastors may make ordinances precisely to maintain order in community life but not for the reasons outlined above.[52] Paul's advice to the Corinthians (in 1 Corinthians 11:5 [head-covering for women] and 14:30-33 [taking turns in the assembly]) served as examples. Such regulations were "for the sake of love and peace" and "to keep order," and they required obedience to bishops and pastors. For Melanchthon, the two limitations outlined above still obtained (par. 56): "However, consciences should not be burdened by holding that such things are necessary for salvation or by considering it a sin when they are violated without giving offense to others."[53]

Having spelled out the positive use of church regulations, Melanchthon made the case that the change in the Sabbath was not something the church had enacted on its own. Rather, this was done away with in Scripture and not by the church. Moreover, worshiping on Sunday was proof of Christian freedom and helped order the church's life. The error in debates over the Sabbath came from the false impression that the church had to replace Levitical and Jewish worship forms with new, required forms also necessary for salvation. Melanchthon even dismissed the notion, held by some scholastic theologians, that the change in the Sabbath, though not strictly speaking divine law, could be treated "as if" it were divine law. "But what else are such debates except snares of conscience?" he wondered, using a particularly pointed form of rhetoric (par. 64). Even promises to mitigate such rules foundered on the claim that the rules themselves were necessary for salvation.[54] In fact, the problem with episcopal regulation went to the core of the gospel: "Now this opinion will persist as long as no one knows anything about the righteousness of faith and Christian freedom."

Melanchthon introduced the parallel issue concerning the authority of the Jerusalem Council and its prohibition of abstaining from blood and what has been strangled precisely because it proved his point regarding Christian freedom and the gospel. In a society that cherished its blood sausage (*Blutwurst*), Melanchthon could simply ask (par. 65), "But who observes this now?" It was not a permanent decree meant to burden consciences. Indeed (par. 66), "the general intention of the gospel [*perpetua voluntas evangelii*] must be considered in connection with the decree." This single sentence summarized the heart of the debate: the primacy of the gospel in debates over church practice and episcopal authority.

As added proof for Melanchthon's relativizing conciliar decrees, he trotted out the example of canon law itself, where (par. 67) "many of [its] rules fall daily into complete disuse." Key for Melanchthon was the proper use of what the reformers loved to call by the Greek term *epieikeia* (here in the German, *Linderung*, and in the Latin, *aequitas*, meaning "balance" or "moderation"); such canons are not necessary and may be disregarded when no harm is done to consciences. This double-edged condition marked the absolute limit of episcopal (or pastoral) authority in the church. No regulation could claim to be necessary for salvation; any regulation could be disregarded (or imposed) as long as no harm was done to consciences.

Taken in this light, Melanchthon's conclusion to the entire *confutatio* (pars. 30–68) could straightforwardly promise obedience to bishops (par. 69) "if they did not insist on the observance of ordinances that cannot be observed without sin." However, the list of such offending ordinances lay at the heart of the Saxon proposal for reconciliation (par. 70): communion in one kind (Article 22), celibate priests (Article 23), and requiring clergy "to swear an oath not to preach this doctrine [outlined in Articles 1–21 and 24], even though it is undoubtedly in accord with the holy gospel." At issue was not the bishops' "honor and dignity" (par. 71), but a plea to "relax certain unreasonable burdens" (par. 72). Melanchthon even conceded that there might well have been reason to impose these regulations at the time (par. 73), despite the fact that many were not well understood (par. 74). Instead, he begged that the bishops, following the example of canon law itself, temper or mitigate (German, *miltern*, and Latin, *mitigare*, again synonyms for *epieikeia*) these ordinances so as not to destroy church unity. Otherwise, the evangelicals would have no choice but to follow the apostolic rule and to obey God rather than mortals (par. 75, referring to Acts 5:29), as Article 26 had already intimated might happen.[55]

Peroratio (76–78, *BC 2000*, 102–3). Although Melanchthon's defense in Article 28 lacked a proper *exordium*, he did give it a rather polished *peroration*, in the form of a summary and a dire warning.[56] Saint Peter himself (1 Peter 5:2) forbade tyranny by church leaders (par. 76). The present question did not require any lessening of episcopal power (now defined in terms of the gospel and eternal righteousness and not in terms of civil righteousness), but rather held an appeal *not* to force consciences to sin (par. 77, German), which Melanchthon defined in the Latin version more precisely as to "permit the teaching of the gospel in its purity

[Articles 1–21] and relax those few observances that cannot be kept without sin [Articles 22–27, especially 22–24]," in other words, the Saxon peace proposal. If the bishops (one cannot help but think he had the papal legate Campeggio and the primate of Germany, Albrecht of Brandenburg, especially in mind) dismissed this petition, "let them consider how they will have to answer to God, since by their obstinacy they cause division and schism, which they should rightly help to prevent."[57]

THE CENTRAL ARGUMENTS OF ARTICLE 28

This detailed rhetorical analysis yields new clarity about the intentions and limitations of Article 28. First, it cannot be said that Lutherans in Augsburg rejected the authority of bishops. Oversight in the church, as in civil affairs, was a wonderful gift of God. The reduction of church order to some sort of federated congregationalism was never the goal of the reformers, and they never envisioned such an entity. Some have argued that, in the "emergency" of the Reformation, episcopal authority was abrogated in favor of a presbyteral organization of the church and that this emergency, having ended, could permit the reinstitution of true, historical episcopal structure back to the Lutheran church. Even this seemingly peace-loving proposal misses the true point in Article 28. The office of bishop and episcopal authority (*episkopé*), far from being under attack, might seem rather to have been rescued by the Augustana. By identifying the office of bishop with preaching the gospel and administering the sacraments, Article 28 in one stroke re-formed the episcopal office in line with the ancient church and under the gospel itself.

Second, as a direct consequence of the first point, Article 28 dismissed out of hand the alternative definitions of episcopal power (standing over civil authority; able to make new regulations necessary for true worship of God) in favor of a definition compatible with the doctrine of justification itself as defined in Article 5—that is, a definition arising from service to the gospel. This meant, as Melanchthon stated in the Apology 28.20 (in both the May and September 1531 Latin editions and in the German translation of Justus Jonas), that obedience to leaders (Hebrews 13:17) "does not create an authority for bishops apart from the gospel. Bishops must not create traditions contrary to the gospel nor interpret their traditions in a manner contrary to the gospel." Both parts of Article 28, the one dealing with the confusion of political and evangelical authority (pars. 1–29) and the one dealing with ecclesial regulations (pars. 30–75) make clear that, *when the gospel itself is at stake,* Christians dare not submit to wayward episcopal authority.[58] But then, they may not submit to wayward presbyteral or congregational authority either.

Third, this close association of episcopal authority to the gospel also means that the consciences of the weak demand special care. Confusion of civil and ecclesial authority threatens the comfort of consciences, as does confusing human regulations in the church with obtaining grace or committing mortal sin.[59] The word *conscience* here must not be restricted to its medieval usage, as a faculty of the soul. Indeed, it might better be construed as "the believer under attack" or "the weak in need of comfort." This comfort is nothing less than the result of the gospel, and hence, the proper function of the episcopal and pastoral office, as Article 20 makes abundantly clear.

Fourth, Melanchthon did not distinguish pastors and bishops. In fact, on several occasions in this article, he lumps the two together.[60] However, rather than leading to a denigration of the episcopal office, it resulted in the raising of the pastoral office to its proper, ancient level. In this regard, it is important to note that the word used in paragraph 53 is not *ministri* (which included preachers and teachers), but *pastores* in the Latin text or *Pfarrer* in the German.[61] The reason Melanchthon on occasion associated the two terms was precisely because the evangelical authority of bishops is nothing other than pastoral: to comfort the terrified conscience with the gospel. Thus, the initial definition of the evangelical bishop in paragraph 5 exactly parallels the language of Article 5. Moreover, paragraph 8 added the connection that some bishops (now evangelically defined) exercise their office over a few, while others exercise it over many, according to their calling (*Beruf, vocatio*). This means that the only difference between pastors and bishops is their specific calling, not their office.

This unity of office and diversity of calling may also assist the church in its present debates over the historic succession of bishops. On the one hand, there must be a historic succession of the gospel (best called true, apostolic succession) that encompasses the entire public office of ministry and does not (indeed, cannot) pit one specific calling against another. It is, instead, precisely the preaching of the gospel and the administration of the sacraments. On the other hand, there can also be, connected to a specific calling of bishops, specific characteristics of oversight (supported by Titus 1:5) and of a historic succession that adheres to the specific call and not necessarily to the underlying evangelical office. This characteristic, like all the others discussed in Article 28, falls under the judgment of the gospel itself and can never be invoked in opposition to that gospel. Only as it serves the good order of the church—in this case, the ecumenical good order of the church—and its gospel can the church continue to cherish it. In fact, if it ceases to serve either, such historic succession always ends up undermining the very unity it was designed to protect. This encapsulates precisely Melanchthon's closing warning (par. 78).

Finally, the twin goals of church order and appropriate Christian freedom actually worked together for Melanchthon. If the goal of any regulation in the church was to maintain good order for the peace and love of the community, then Christian freedom to change regulations or to maintain them remained intact. Only when ordinances led to the servitude under the law or to the crushing of consciences did a God-given reason to resist the church's proper pastoral or episcopal authorities arise. This substantially narrows the possible reasons for defying "the [ecclesiastical] system" and means that the burden of proof for resisting episcopal authority (oversight) must always rest where Melanchthon put it: on the shoulders of the one resisting. In

Article 28, the one resisting was Melanchthon himself, and so he had to muster the best logical and rhetorical arguments to make his case. In this way, Article 28, more than any other article, rested upon the confession of faith in Articles 1–21. This means that in the Lutheran churches, one must first demonstrate that a bishop or an episcopal form of governance or an ecumenical agreement contradicts the gospel itself before one can counsel people to oppose it or their bishops. Arguments from tradition—whether from the ancient church or from the more recent past—hold no water. If a practice maintains good order in the church and does not contradict the gospel's freedom by making the practice necessary for salvation (!), then well-meaning Christians cannot object to its institution.

Chapter 5

Witnessing to the Evangelical Office of Bishop in *The Book of Concord*

Lutheran discussion of the episcopal office did not end with Article 28 of the Augsburg Confession. In fact, we find two other lengthy expositions of the office of bishop in *The Book of Concord*. In the Apology, we again discover Philip Melanchthon's rhetorical genius at work, as he was forced to respond to his Roman opponents. In the Treatise on the Power and Primacy of the Pope, intended as an appendix to the Augsburg Confession, we witness how he used logic and classroom skills to explain both the reformers' criticisms of the papacy and the acceptance of oversight.

The Apology 28

For the most part, comments about bishops from the Apology have been woven into the examination of Article 28 of the Augsburg Confession (see chapters 3 and 4). However, two passages hold special interest. The first, Apology 28.59–60 (*BC 2000*, 255–56), contains Melanchthon's refutation of the charge of schism on the grounds of the evangelicals' disobedience of the Roman bishops. Its method of argumentation, completely foreign to some modern Lutheran debates, shows just how carefully he distinguished civil and evangelical righteousness in his understanding of church order. He began by distinguishing obedience to regular bishops with "casting aside the clear truth":

We know we are laying ourselves open to the charge of schism because we seem to have separated ourselves from those who are regarded as the regular bishops. But our consciences are very much at ease since we know that while we most earnestly want to establish harmony, it is not possible to please our opponents without casting aside the clear truth.

It would seem at first glance that *any* truth claim would give a person leave to abandon episcopal (or any other) rule in the church. However, what follows demonstrates that Melanchthon delineated truth claims very carefully. The opposite of truth in this case was injustice, dissolution of marriage, murder, exile, and the orphaning of children. Melanchthon wrote:

We would have to go along with the opponents in the defense of this unjust law, the dissolution of existing marriages, the murder of priests who refuse to submit, the exile of poor women and orphaned children. But since it is well established that these actions displease God, we can in no way have an alliance with the multitude of murderers among the opponents.

Thus, it is the clear breaking of natural and civil law that stood against the truth, not just Melanchthon's own opinion about the celibacy of priests—that is, it was in the first instance a clear argument from civil righteousness. Even his summary did not mention the gospel, but instead talked about divine and natural law, canon law, superstition, and fraud. He claimed that religious arguments were just an evil pretext for oppression:

It conflicts with divine and natural law; it disagrees with the canons themselves; it is superstitious and very dangerous; and, finally, the entire thing is a fraud. The real purpose of the law is not religion but domination, for which religion is just a wicked pretext. Neither can sane people bring anything forward against these very firmly established arguments.

By contrast, it is not at all clear that any argument in current debates over episcopal authority, especially regarding exclusive ordination by bishops, rises to this level. For Melanchthon, the claim to truth could never simply be an argument from one's own logic but had to stand on clear principles of justice. Claims to historical succession, while perhaps foolish or unnecessary, never have been shown to involve ipso facto assaults on human rights and justice.

The other major discussion of bishops comes, of course, in Apology 28. This article follows very strictly the rules of rhetoric. Once again, knowing this fact will help clarify the overall thrust of Melanchthon's argument. Rather than treat these comments as a treasure trove of theological aphorisms, each separated from the next, Melanchthon's own books on rhetorical method would instruct us differently, as we already observed in chapter 4, where the reader will also find definitions of these technical terms.

Exordium *(Apology 28.1–5;* BC 2000, *289)*

Already in the beginning of the article, Melanchthon quickly dismissed the objections raised by the *confutatio* (refutation). The opponents were worried about the "privileges and immunities of the ecclesiastical state." Melanchthon could care less, and called the objections sheer slander. "For in this article, we were arguing about other things" (Apology 28.2, in *BC 2000*, 289). Moreover, such privileges were political matters granted by princes and not at issue.

There follows (pars. 3–5) the more classical *exordium*. Having dismissed the paltry arguments of the opponents (he would come back to more serious issues in his own confutation below), Melanchthon now appealed to the hearts of the readers in quite moving language. He portrayed the complaints of the churches and pious hearts. He sketched the opponents' love of riches and neglect of the church, especially the gospel, in favor of their own traditions. Now, in the present controversies, instead of offering direction to the people, the opponents "issue a call to arms" and "an edict written in blood." Melanchthon begged them to "see the tears of the sufferers and hear the pitiful complains of many good people," complaints that God himself hears.

STATUS CONTROVERSIAE: *THE CHIEF ARGUMENT AT THE HEART OF THE CONTROVERSY (APOLOGY 28.6;* BC 2000, *289)*

With this very "hot" introduction (perhaps some of the most dramatic prose of the Apology), Melanchthon then restated (in par. 6 [*BC 2000*, 289]) the "issue at the heart of the controversy," one that sharply defined the office of bishop in evangelical terms and rejected out of hand the objections in the *confutatio*. Despite the fact that Article 28 of the Augsburg Confession dealt with several issues (actually, two, as we saw in chapter 4), the opponents made the following (for Melanchthon, outrageous) claim. "Bishops have . . . the power to rule and to correct by force in order to guide their subjects toward the goal of eternal bliss, and that the power to rule requires the power to judge, to define, to distinguish, and to determine what is helpful or conducive to the aforementioned goal." Thus, as Melanchthon saw it, the question had now been narrowed to whether "bishops have the power to create laws useful for attaining eternal life." One gets the feeling that he could not have been happier to argue this point.

CONFIRMATIO *(APOLOGY 28.7–18A;* BC 2000, *289–91)*

In the *confirmatio* (proof of one's own position) that follows (pars. 7–18), Melanchthon rehearsed arguments familiar to any reader of the Augsburg Confession. He first (par. 7) distinguished the free forgiveness of sins in Christ from human traditions, which are worthless to earn salvation. Using Matthew 15:11 and Romans 14:17 to create a syllogism (actually an enthymeme), he came to the expected conclusion (par. 8 in *BC 2000*, 290): "Therefore, bishops have no right to create traditions in addition to the gospel as though they merited the forgiveness of sins or were acts of worship that God approves as righteousness and that burden consciences in such a way that their omission would be a sin." He again used Acts 15 (par. 8) as a single proof for the apostolicity of his arguments.

He also tied his opponents' condemnation of Article 15 (on human tradition) to this argument. As if wearied of syllogistic argumentation, he posed (in par. 9) a series of rhetorical questions to dismiss the notion that human traditions merit eternal life and concluded with a reference to Colossians 2:20-23 (par. 10 in *BC 2000*, 290).[1] By using such a rhetorical device here, he offered two conclusions that sent the ball back into the opponents' court. "So let the opponents explain how traditions are useful for winning eternal life." That was the first half of his argument. The second half (par. 11 in *BC 2000*, 290), which mentioned bishops specifically and arose out of the gospel's clear rejection of human traditions as a way of salvation, was equally pointed: "Therefore the opponents will never be able to show that bishops have the power to institute such acts of worship."

If Melanchthon's first argument touched on the relation of traditions to the gospel, his second honed in on the definition of bishop itself. Here, he made it clear that he was not talking about those named bishops "according to canonical law," but about those who were bishops "according to the gospel." Upon this distinction rests much of his argument. Melanchthon simply refused to discuss questions of canon law. That law, which required that bishops be in communion with Rome and thereby to be under Rome's claim to apostolic succession, was a simple adiaphoron, not worth arguing about. The same is still true today. If some find this tradition important for the good order of the church and the (human) blessings that may accrue thereby, well and good. The question for today's Lutherans *must* remain the gospel and *evangelical* bishops and pastors. Anyone can be in historic succession with someone or another (with a bishop, a presbyter, a congregation, a person, or even oneself)—or even in doctrinal succession! But preaching the gospel and administering the sacraments according to the gospel is another thing altogether.

To explain this distinction further, Melanchthon hearkened back to an old legal distinction between office and jurisdiction (pars. 13–14). The office (Latin, *ordo*) of bishop is to preach, teach, and administer the sacraments. The power of jurisdiction pertained directly to the authority to excommunicate flagrant sinners and to receive back the penitent. Such jurisdiction, as Melanchthon never wearied of saying, did not give bishops authorization to act as tyrants (as if there were no law) or as monarchs (as if they were above the law). This jurisdictional right did not give them the authority to enact new acts of worship, but gave only the authority to preach and teach according to the gospel and to correct those who do not.

Having introduced this distinction, Melanchthon was forced to admit that bishops *did* have the jurisdictional right to introduce traditions into the church, but (par. 15 in *BC 2000*, 291) "for preserving order in the church for the sake of peace." He continued: "These must not ensnare consciences." This phrase, once again, strikes near the heart of the Lutheran witness to the gospel and its effect: comfort. The comfort of the terrified conscience trumps every jurisdictional claim of every pastor, because it goes to the core of the pastoral and episcopal office. This comfort frees from enslavement to traditions and from claims to inerrancy or infallibility, whether they rest on episcopal claims to apostolic succession or on a pious construal of a democratized priesthood of all believers and congregational autonomy.

Here, and not in discussions of church order, is where Paul's call to freedom from Galatians 5:1 belongs: "For freedom Christ has set us free. Stand firm, therefore, and do not submit again to a yoke of slavery." Thus, Melanchthon concluded with a simple rule, which could still inform modern church life (par. 16 in *BC 2000*, 291): "Therefore the use of such ordinances ought to be left free, with the stipulation that offenses should be avoided and that they not be regarded as required acts of worship." The apostles ordained many things in their day that no longer applied in Melanchthon's. Similarly, the Reformation churches set up many things that no longer apply in ours. And many of our concerns will be passé to future generations. This remarkable freedom that Melanchthon showed here is a lesson that Lutheran churches have yet to learn, as they forever imagine that some tradition or another (or some completely new teaching or practice) will rescue the church. This (par. 17 in *BC 2000*, 291) "simple rule for interpreting traditions," respected (par. 18 in *BC 2000*, 291) by many "great and learned people," provided Melanchthon a last word of the *confirmatio* and an introduction to the *confutatio* (answer to opponents' arguments). "We do not see what possible objection there can be to this."

CONFUTATIO *(APOLOGY 28.18B–24C;* BC 2000, *291–93)*

Melanchthon had already announced in the exordium that the objections of the Roman party (contained in the document called the *Confutation*) were meaningless. However, this was somewhat disingenuous, insofar as he actually had to deal seriously with several points that the opponents had used in their attack. Three biblical texts and the charge of undermining public order (already introduced in Apology 28) claimed Melanchthon's attention.

Luke 10:16 ("Whoever listens to you listens to me") stated one of the most important objections to the evangelicals—so important that Emser's printer put this text in the mouth of Jesus on the cover of his version of the German New Testament from 1527, so that it served as a Roman answer to Luther's translation of the New Testament. The accompanying woodcut depicted the Lord handing authority to Peter and Paul (and mutatis mutandis their successors). Melanchthon dismissed this charge with little more than a wave of his hand. Jesus spoke these words against traditionalists, not in their favor (par. 18 in *BC 2000*, 291). Rather than giving apostles unlimited authority, the passage gave testimony that we can believe them *not* regarding their own words but as giving testimony to another's word, namely the word of Christ. The "listen to me" (par. 19 in *BC 2000*, 291) requires the apostles to teach in such a way that the people hear Christ himself. Even in today's church, this should be the primary thing. Melanchthon concluded with a huff: "Therefore, [Christ] wants his voice, his Word, to be heard, not human traditions. Thus these jackasses take a statement that supports our position and contains the profoundest kind of comfort and teaching, and they misapply it to such trifles as the distinction of foods and clothing and the like."[2]

In the second instance (par. 20), Hebrews 13:17 ("Obey your leaders"), Melanchthon deftly added the underlying presupposition: provided that they teach the gospel. To show that, using the logic of his day, the opponents' argumentation included an "undistributed middle," Melanchthon employed the word of Paul in Galatians 1:8, a Bible passage so important to the evangelical side that Luther used it in the letters he wrote to the emperor and the imperial estates after the Diet of Worms.[3]

Melanchthon pointed out that the third text, Matthew 23:3, where Jesus commands obedience to the Pharisees and scribes, was the same as the second, and he contrasted it to Acts 5:29, the text that already figured in Article 16, as the one exception to obeying civil magistrates. If—and (one has to express today Melanchthon's unspoken supposition) only if—bishops teach evil things, one must not obey them. Recalling the chief arguments in Article 28 and in the *confirmatio*, Melanchthon concluded (par. 21 in *BC 2000*, 292): "But these are wicked things: that human traditions are the worship of God; that they are required acts of worship; that they merit the forgiveness of sins and eternal life."

Far more serious is the final objection, one that occasionally plagues Christians today, namely, that evangelical teaching caused civil unrest. The Roman opponents placed responsibility for the Peasants' War at the feet of the reformers. Not satisfied with his original answer in the Apology from May 1531, Melanchthon completely rewrote this section for the September version.[4] At stake was the entire Reformation. If it could be shown that evangelical doctrine destroyed people and undermined civil peace and good order, then the evangelicals' refusal to obey bishops (or at least to put up with them) would have been a sham, a cover for civil unrest.

The care with which Melanchthon answered these objections revealed the crux of his theology. First, he pointed out the obvious: there was more order and peace in Lutheran lands than anywhere else.[5] Second, and by far more important, Melanchthon excused any scandals on the basis of the two doctrines upon which he had anchored Article 28 of the Augsburg Confession in the first place: (1) that we receive forgiveness of sins and are accounted righteous freely on account of Christ by faith and not because of works, and (2) that a prince's laws and the political structures come from God and exist for a Christian to use for the good. Yet, as was always Melanchthon's practice, the definition of a thing always led to a discussion of its effects. Paragraph 23 in *BC 2000*, 292, reads: "For frightened consciences can have no firm consolation against God's wrath unless the first article [justification] is known. The second article [political obedience] greatly preserves political tranquility." What was at stake was the doctrine that lies at the heart of Melanchthon's own theology and that of Wittenberg: the distinction between the twofold righteousness of God and its effects: divine consolation and earthly tranquility.

By contrast, the opponents taught neither doctrine in their books and, moreover, suppressed both. Thus, they, and not the evangelical party, had most contributed to social and theological unrest. While many originally praised Luther for his writings on this subject—Melanchthon was probably thinking of *On Secular Authority* of 1523—they later condemn him. Even the Greek poet Pindar, whom Melanchthon cited in the original Greek, had predicted such fickle behavior.[6] In the spirit of a true *confutatio*, Melanchthon turned the table on his opponents and blamed them for the empire's unrest. By condemning Luther in the first place (1521), by persecuting good people, and by rousing the people against the reformers, the opponents had played into the devil's hands. Although public unrest bothered the evangelical side, they dared not offend Christ by following the demands of the bishops.

The bishops' behavior in trying to suppress the evangelical witness to the gospel and to blame them for unrest was simply one more trick up the devil's sleeve to bring the gospel itself into disrepute. Finally, Melanchthon turned up the rhetorical heat and provided a catalogue of the opposition's worst offenses: the sacrifice of the Mass, forced celibacy, worship of saints, papal power grabs, sale of benefices, theological inanities and exegetical fabrications, monkish superstitions, and, worst of all, suppression of the gospel and its teachers. This was simply the fulfillment of Revelation, Melanchthon mentioned in passing, an oblique reference to the papacy as Antichrist. In a final rhetorical flourish, Melanchthon apologized for listing these things—forced as he was by the *confutatio*'s lack of respect for God's word.

PERORATIO *(APOLOGY 28.24C–27,* BC 2000, *193–94)*

In a seamless continuation of the foregoing, Melanchthon launched into a peroration (not just for Article 28, but for the entire Apology), especially calling upon his two "judges" (the emperor and the reader) for clemency and a fair hearing.[7] He again stated the evangelicals' desire for peace and added how much they respected the emperor himself, endowed as he was "with heroic virtues." However, invoking again the so-called *clausula Petri* of Acts 5:29 ("We ought to obey God rather than mortals"), Melanchthon explained that the gospel trumped every other authority. Instead, the persecution of the gospel and the evangelicals who bore witness to it brought the burden for dividing the church back upon the Roman side.

The overall thrust of Melanchthon's arguments in Apology 28 is clear. When talking about bishops today, one must still distinguish the twofold righteousness of God: the one for maintaining order in the church and the world; the other for consoling the terrified with the forgiveness of sins. No matter what else Lutherans might say about the episcopal office, they must say these two things.

The Lutheran Appendix to the Confessio Augustana: The Treatise

The Treatise on the Power and Primacy of the Pope—conceived as an appendix to the Augsburg Confession, written under the shadow of the papal call for a council (that did not take place until 1545 in Trent), and composed within a single week by Philip Melanchthon—has all the marks of Melanchthon's *loci* method and demonstrates not so much the rhetorical sophistication found in the Augsburg Confession or Apology as the dialectical rigor of Wittenberg's classroom. Because it was conceived as an appendix to the Confession, Melanchthon did not repeat the argumentation found there except to state expressly (par. 60) that this document did not contradict what he had already stated there on the question of ecclesiastical power.

PART 1: REJECTING PAPAL TYRANNY *(TPPP 1–59;* BC 2000, *330–40)*

The fact that Melanchthon first mentioned the Augsburg Confession at paragraph 60 indicates, however, that the opening arguments were indeed new. Faced with the possibility of a council for which the evangelical party had been calling since at least 1520 in Luther's famous *Address to the Christian Nobility,* the evangelicals now had to explain why they could not attend a council controlled by the pope. It was not so much the idea of a pope to which Melanchthon objected as it was specifically to the claims that the papacy made about itself.

Following the rules of what Melanchthon conceived of as classroom rhetoric, which used syllogisms and logic instead of emotional appeals, he first stated the three papal claims: superiority over all other pastors and bishops; power over both secular and ecclesial powers; and the necessity—on pain of losing salvation—to believe these very things. Then, after asserting the evangelical position (par. 4 in *BC 2000,* 330) that these things were "false, impious, tyrannical and ruinous to the church," Melanchthon defined these three topics in more detail (pars. 5–6), where in this case definition (*finitio*) provided the basic building blocks for all logical argumentation. In what follows (pars. 7–59), Melanchthon systematically went through the three claims and proved the contrary based upon both Scripture and tradition.

Only in the context of this very narrowly conceived argument against papal hegemony can Melanchthon's argument be understood. Otherwise, one runs the risk of taking his arguments against *papal* usurpation of power and using them to defend a similar usurpation of power by pastors, congregations, or even individuals. Melanchthon had no interest in writing against an office of oversight in the church, which was by 1537 well on the way to full development in many evangelical territories of the empire. Instead, he was composing arguments to be used against the tyranny of papal power grabbing. The same arguments can be used against other groups in the church only to the extent that those groups show the same kind of pretensions: claiming to exercise authority for all others in the church (for example, by claiming that *all* authority in the church rests in and derives from the laity), claiming to have ultimate authority in politics and ecclesiastical affairs, and insisting that such things are matters of faith (and, therefore, not adiaphora).

The arguments against papal primacy over pastors and bishops take up the largest portion of the first part of the tract, stretching from paragraphs 7 to 30. Melanchthon offered two different kinds of proof to undercut the papal claim: first from Scripture (pars. 7–11) and then from history (pars. 12–20). He then answered the anticipated objections of his opponents (pars. 21–30) in the kind of *confutatio* that one would expect from such classroom rhetoric, dealing especially with the two *loci classici* (classic proof texts) already handled seventeen years earlier by Luther in his fights with Jerome Emser.

The positive arguments most clearly outlined a case for the servant-leadership that Melanchthon envisioned for the church. Luke 22:22-27 forbids lordship in the church. Apostles, pastors, and bishops are equally servants and never lords. Similarly, passages from Jesus' commissioning of the apostles (John 20:21) and from Paul (Galatians 2:6 and 1 Corinthians 3:4-8; 3:21-22) make the same point. Paragraph 11 (in *BC 2000*, 331) reads: "Paul regards all ministers as equals and teaches that the church is superior to its ministers." The problem is domination, in whatever form it may occur.

The historical evidence served the same end. What is worth noting here is that Melanchthon wished to prove two things: first, that the bishop of Rome was the equal of other bishops during the early history of the church, and second, that the consecration of bishops took place with the consent of local bishops—the very practice that the evangelicals tried (unsuccessfully, in the end) to follow at the installations of the first evangelical bishops in Naumburg (Nicholas von Amsdorff) and Merseburg (Georg von Anhalt). The citation of Cyprian is particularly interesting, since it accepted, without comment, the continuing role of bishops in the life and governance of the church ("by the vote of the whole body and the decision of the bishops gathered in their presence, the episcopal office was entrusted to him with the laying on of hands"). It was not democracy but a balance between the agreement of the people who knew him best and the neighboring bishops who decide. Melanchthon's method of argumentation tried to overwhelm the reader with proofs: from Cyprian, Augustine, Jerome, conciliar decisions, and even Pope Gregory I.

This set up a brief discussion of the objectionable biblical passages, especially Matthew 16, which Melanchthon interpreted as a special case of Matthew 18, treating Peter as a representative for all of the apostles and interpreting the "rock" in verse 18 as not Peter but Peter's ministry. This approach, slightly different from Luther's (who, like Chrysostom, had argued that the "rock" was Peter's faith), allowed Melanchthon to introduce one of the reformers' favorite themes on this matter: that the differences among various members of Christ's body are not a matter of a separate estate (*Stand*) but of office (*Amt*). Moreover, while quoting Chrysostom accurately (par. 28), Melanchthon used what the church father said not to argue the exegetical case but to prove that the fathers did not use this text to prove Peter's superiority. For Melanchthon, the point was ministry—where, once again he used "ministry" in its original meaning as "service of the Word" and "faith in that Word." Similarly, John 21:17 was dismissed out of hand, since "feeding sheep" was not about authority but about ministry of the Word and governance in the church. Thus Melanchthon argued not that there should not be bishops or oversight in the church, but rather that all oversight must serve the gospel and the people of God created by the gospel.

The centrality of ministry, understood as service to the gospel, was underscored as Melanchthon turned to the second papal claim: that of political authority. The clarity of Melanchthon's rebuttal highlighted the centrality of his definition of the episcopal and pastoral office:

> Christ gave to his apostles only spiritual authority, that is, the command to preach the gospel, to proclaim the forgiveness of sins, to administer the sacraments, and to excommunicate the ungodly without the use of physical force. He did not give them the power of the sword or the right to establish, take possession or dispose of the kingdoms of the world.[8]

To this definition Melanchthon immediately combined biblical proof texts in favor of his arguments (Matthew 28:19-20; John 20:21) and against the usurpation of political authority (John 18:36; 2 Corinthians 1:24 and 10:4). As a historical example, he pitted Christ being crowned with thorns and robed in purple prior to his crucifixion against the "false and impious" claims of Pope Boniface VIII, the medieval pope whose decrees most clearly defended papal monarchy. This same contrast had already taken visible shape for the Wittenbergers in 1521 in the harshly polemical series of woodcuts *Passional of Christ and Antichrist*, for which Luther and Melanchthon had prepared satirical subtexts.[9] Now Melanchthon used it to attack hundreds of years of papal meddling in imperial politics (pars. 34–36). The actual meddling, he concluded, was not nearly as bad as the spiritual justification for it: using Christ as a pretext for such actions and claiming that it was necessary for salvation to believe such tyranny. Thus, the real reason for rejecting these claims was the damage done to faith and, by extension, to the gospel itself.

This ferocious usurpation of power in this world happened not just to Roman popes but to all kinds of self-appointed keepers of the public good and morals. The biggest disservice we could do to the Treatise would be to limit its warning to the Italian papacy of the sixteenth century and beyond—good for Luther's day but of little use in our own, when the pope rules only a few acres outside Rome and world leaders court his favor but shun his advice. There are many other ways in today's society to build the equivalent to Boniface VIII's "Omnes." When pastors keep their congregants' consciences bound to the pastors' own moral opinions; when congregations demand that pastors and bishops be little more than hired hands and censure them for pointing out the political ramifications of Christian faith; when pastors, bishops, or entire churches claim to be anything more than faithful Christians fulfilling their vocations in the world: then the same kind of tyranny and confusion of faith and Christ's reign with political success threaten the church.

When Melanchthon took up the third papal claim, he began this section with an interesting turn of argumentation. With his actual German opponents in mind, some of whom also questioned the authority of the papacy (over against a general council), Melanchthon conceded, for the sake of argument, the divine authority of the papacy. Even if his earlier arguments were wrong (which, of course, Melanchthon did not think was the case), there still was no reason to obey popes who supported ungodly worship, idolatry, and false doctrine. Next to two of the evangelicals' favorite biblical proof texts (Galatians 1:8 and Acts 5:29), Melanchthon added the example of the apostles, who did not obey Caiaphas.

This was the point of the entire section (pars. 38–49): Christians and the Christian church could never tolerate bad teaching and practice. In this connection, Melanchthon cautiously suggested that this is how the papacy fulfilled the criteria for Antichrist that Saint Paul described in 2 Thessalonians (2:4). There, according to Melanchthon, Paul described not a foreign ruler (that is, the Turkish Sultan) but someone ruling in the church as the creator of false doctrine and claimant of divine rule. Melanchthon then showed how the pope fulfilled all three conditions (par. 40).

Therefore (par. 41), Christians should then take care not to associate themselves with such a ruler on the basis of both Matthew 7:15 ("Beware of false prophets") and 2 Corinthians 6:14 ("Do not be mismatched with unbelievers"). This is a crucial turn in the argument, for underneath the refusal to attend a council controlled by the pope lurked the charge of schism. Until the moment a general council was held, despite all other indications to the contrary, the evangelicals could easily deflect the charge of schism in the church. Now, faced with such a council, they had to give good reason why they were not going to attend. This position actually has enormous consequences for ecumenism, despite initial contrary impressions. This sets the bar for rejection of ecumenism or walking out of a church extremely high. If, and only if, the one who controls such a meeting is Antichrist does an evangelical Christian have reason not to attend or not to remain in communion with another person or group. Rule in the church, ungodly doctrine, *and* claims of divine right to rule must all converge before one can remain outside such a gathering.

To prove just how serious their case against the pope was, Melanchthon then listed (pars. 43–49), in unusually sharp language, the forms of idolatrous practice and false teaching that exist. Abuses of the Mass, the teaching about penance, the practice of indulgences, the invocation of saints, forced celibacy for priests: all were idolatrous. "Truly they do harm to the glory of Christ and bring souls to ruin" (par. 48 in *BC 2000*, 338). Added to this, the pope both enforced these things with cruelty and refused to allow the church freely to judge—a position of the curialists finally approved by Vatican I but already present in the canon law of Melanchthon's day. In this "double tyranny," the latter was worse by far. Paragraph 49 (in *BC 2000*, 338) reads: "For when the church has been deprived of valid judicial process, it is not possible to remove ungodly teachings and impious forms of worship, and they destroy countless souls generation upon generation."

Here one again might want to reduce Melanchthon's comments to anger against the papacy. However, the temptation he described exists at all levels in the church, wherever people— pastors, congregations, individuals, bishops, or even theological professors—imagine themselves to be above reproach and beyond the reach of the admonition by other Christians. That is, when service—*Dienerschaft* or *ministerium*—no longer defines Christian ministry, there is always and only Antichrist the destruction of countless souls.

In the conclusion to this third section, Melanchthon shifted gears and called upon Christian princes to intervene. At first read-ing, this section may seem especially alien to a world in which most governments have little or no interest in Christianity and where some even eschew all connections between church and society. What did Melanchthon mean by allowing princes into the church? In fact, however, Melanchthon was appealing to those with authority in the world who were also members of the church. Paying attention to his precise method of arguing actually helps clarify how to broaden the applicability of this section of the Trea-tise. First, he began, one should consider (par. 52) the "great errors and tyranny" of papal rule and how appearing neutral (as many church officials, learned people, and princes in Germany were still doing) actually was no different from abetting a murderer.

Second, he appealed directly to Christian princes and kings to fulfill their calling, which by 1537 meant for both Melanchthon and Luther (par. 54 in *BC 2000*, 339) to "promote the glory of God." This care of religion (*cura religionis*), often ignored or misunderstood by historians, formed a crucial part of the developing Reformation—*not* because the reformers were enamored of princes (rare birds in heaven) but because princes alone had the power in society to prevent idolatry.[10] In a world wracked by globalization, we only wring our hands and wish that someone with the power to intervene would confront, in the name of justice, the idols of power, wealth, and oppression that threaten our world. Many churches still include people of power, and yet theologians are sometimes loath to equip them to care for religion in their own callings and offices. Melanchthon was neither as idealistic nor as shortsighted as his Lutheran descendants.

In a final section of the first part of the Treatise, Melanchthon summarized his arguments. Papal cruelty was real; idolatry had to be shunned; there was good reason not to submit to the pope—despite charges of causing schism. Those who ally themselves with the pope, Melanchthon concluded, share in his idolatrous teaching, his persecution of the faithful, his offense to God's glory, and his undermining of the church's well-being. What, he wondered, could be worse than that?

PART 2: EPISCOPAL POWER AND JURISDICTION (TPPP 60–79; BC 2000, 340–43)

In a much shorter section (pars. 60–79), Melanchthon turned to an issue raised in the Augsburg Confession and its Apology: the authority of bishops. By admitting that these subjects were already covered there, he invited later readers to view this document in their light (and not the other way around)—that is, what Melanchthon proposed in the Treatise was not a recantation of the evangelical party's position of 1530–1531 but a clarification of it.

What needed clarification was precisely what had happened in between 1530 and 1537—the wholesale ordination of priests—and later in the 1540s—the consecration of bishops. It was clear, as we have already seen, that the Saxon party and its allies were willing to allow the ordinary bishops to ordain. In fact, few ordinations had taken place before the 1530s.[11] However, by the mid-1530s, the Wittenberg church was ordaining candidates for ministry (either pastoral or preaching positions as well as deacons), conferring doctorates in theology, and (by the 1540s) installing (or as they said, "ordaining") bishops. At first glance, this seems to speak directly to some of the contemporary debates over the episcopal office. However, there is one major difference between the present debates and Melanchthon's arguments.

Where Melanchthon began his argument differs greatly from present discussions. He defined the authority given to "those who preside over the churches" as proclamation of the Word and administration of the sacraments—the same authority given in Article 5 of the Augsburg Confession. He added the legal authority to excommunicate those guilty of public crimes and to absolve those who repent. He then included a sentence (par. 61 in *BC 2000*, 340) that may come as a surprise: "It is universally acknowledged, even by our opponents, that this power is shared by divine right by all who preside in the churches, whether they are called pastors, presbyters or bishops." By reducing the sacraments to two or three (Baptism, the Lord's Supper, and absolution), the standard definition of church and ministry by Word and sacraments applied for the evangelicals to all who preside in the churches. The two rites reserved for bishops (confirmation and ordination) now could be dealt with separately. In the sixteenth century, no one understood what confirmation was, since its connection to Baptism had been completely lost, so it did not really cause much consternation in the evangelical camp. Ordination, however, was the real sticking point.

In the argument over equality of presiding, Jerome was of great help to the reformers. In his letter to Evangelus, Jerome noted the equivalence of bishop (*episcopos*) and elder (*presbyteros*) in Paul's letter to Titus and gave a short history of divergences of practice in this matter. Whatever Jerome's point may have been, Melanchthon used his comments to conclude (par. 63 in *BC 2000*, 340) that "the distinctions of degree between bishop and presbyter or pastor are established by human authority." Now he was ready to argue that episcopal ordination (the real issue here) was a matter of human right, not divine right.

The sentence that has often confused people is the next one (par. 65 in *BC 2000*, 340): "However, since the distinction of rank between bishop and pastor is not by divine right, it is clear that an ordination performed by a pastor in his own church is valid by divine right." First, it is important to note that Melanchthon did not say "any ordained person," but rather "pastor" (German: *Pfarrherr*). Preachers, who were also ordained to their office, and teachers, who were called to their offices, were not mentioned here. In fact, the idea that someone who did *not* preside in a church (which for Melanchthon meant, for example, *the* church of Wittenberg)—that is, who was *not* at least head pastor of a major town or zip code (as one might call it today)—had the right to ordain was the furthest thing from Melanchthon's mind—or those of his readers or the signers of this document.

Indeed, the very next paragraph indicates under what circumstances someone could actually countermand the good order of the church. Such circumstances did not include when one loses a vote, does not like the bishop, or disagrees with some policy, or when one wants to assert the power of the laity over the clergy or of the clergy over bishops. Instead, Melanchthon stated (pars. 66–67 in *BC 2000*, 340–41):

> As a result, when the regular bishops become enemies of the gospel or are unwilling to ordain, the churches retain their right to do so. For wherever the church exists, there also is the right to administer the gospel. Therefore, it is necessary for the church to retain the right to call, choose and ordain ministers.

"When the regular bishops become enemies of the gospel." This one sentence forces anyone who may wish to do away with the regular order of the church to prove their case at the highest possible level. Bishops must be enemies of the gospel or unwilling to ordain. It is no wonder that, until the so-called

Peace of Augsburg of 1555, evangelicals tried to bring bishops and dioceses into the mainstream of the evangelical confession of faith. Moreover, for Melanchthon, the "right" to ordain did not devolve to individuals (pastors) or to groups (the ordained clergy or the laity or the individual congregation). The *church*, as Melanchthon argued in some detail in the following paragraphs,[12] never lost the right to ordain—simply because, as already Article 5 of the Confession made clear, the gospel had to have its public ministers. The mail must get through![13]

"The church," as Melanchthon used the term here, was neither simply an isolated congregation nor a worldwide organization. Church for the reformers was always more event than organization and always encompassed all times and places as the assembly of believers gathered around the events of Word and sacrament. The church had to have, as part of its *essential* offices, public ministers who proclaimed the gospel. This was a necessity. How that ministry might be ordered would vary from place to place. However, there would always be oversight, mutual accountability and service to the assembled believers, and service of the gospel. For Melanchthon, the proof text was Ephesians 4:8-12 (par. 67). Apostles, prophets, and teachers were gifts of Christ to the church. These gifts did not depart from the church, and in an emergency—as with emergency baptisms—anyone might assume the office, not as a right but as a necessity. At this point (pars. 69–70), Melanchthon used 1 Peter 2:9 ("You are a royal priesthood") not as a reference to the laity but as a reference to the entire church, which by virtue of this priesthood could not lose the authority to ordain folks to public ministry.

Again (par. 72 in *BC 2000*, 341), Melanchthon associated this right of the church with its extraordinary exercise under very special circumstances, such as the evangelicals were facing in the 1530s: "Consequently when bishops either become heretical or are unwilling to ordain, the churches are compelled by divine right to ordain pastors and ministers for themselves." There was here no claiming of rights (for laity, clergy, or congregations), but compunction by divine right—indeed, a very strange way to argue. There had to be clear heresy or a complete unwillingness to ordain before churches were compelled to act this way. In such cases, the fault for schism fell, in Melanchthon's eyes, where he had always put it: on the tyrants in the church.

Skipping over confirmation and the blessing of bells, Melanchthon set his sights on the other major abuse of episcopal power: excommunication. Important in the present context was not the practice itself but Melanchthon's chief, indeed only, complaint: tyranny. These paragraphs (74–76 in *BC 2000*, 342) fairly bristled with contempt, using words such as *arbitrary, intolerable license, tyrannical fashion*, and *tyrannically*. This kind of language went to the heart of any discussion of authority in the church: "It shall not be so with you, but whoever would be first must be last . . . must serve." When it came to diocesan marriage courts (pars. 77–78), the key word (outside of the mention that such matters used to be handled by secular authorities, who had a divine command to intervene if the churches failed to act) was *justice*.

Melanchthon summed up the arguments of this second section in a series of logical syllogisms (actually, enthymemes). The result is clear: the evangelicals *had no choice* but to reject these people as bishops.[14] The reasons for disobeying bishops were serious. Melanchthon set the bar extremely high: defense of ungodly teaching and worship; refusal to ordain good pastors; tyranny in the church; injustice among the people; and defrauding the church by failing to fulfill the true, evangelical office of bishop. There was no talk of tradition, of an *Übertragungslehre* (doctrine of transference [of authority from the laity to the pastors]), of presbyteral succession, or of democratic ideals. These and most other present-day arguments seem trivial in the face of idolatry, tyranny, and injustice. The stakes were (and are) eschatologically high, so that Melanchthon ended (par. 82 in *BC 2000*, 343) with a warning from 2 Peter (2:13-15) about leaders arising in the future who would spend alms on luxury and neglect the ministry:

"Therefore, let those who defraud the church know that God will exact punishment for their sin."

In this context, Melanchthon's comments make the most sense. There is, to use a phrase my father was fond of, a kind of "honest graft" at work in the church today. We see it in pastors and bishops who do not preach the gospel of the free forgiveness of sins in Christ because it is not popular or because they did not learn such a message growing up. We find it at work in congregational and synodic councils who mistake programs for proclamation and survival for sacrifice. It is the honest graft of mistaking morality for unconditional grace and the passing popularity of entertainment for the Real Presence. There is a crisis of leadership in today's church, but its subtlety makes it much more difficult to ferret out. Melanchthon's concerns are clear, but the way they arise today may not be.

The Confessional Witness

It is important not to turn the Lutheran Confessions themselves into the kind of papal tyranny they reject. They can be only witnesses to the truth, never tyrants over the truth. Yet, within the parameters of witness, these confessional documents testify to the following things about bishops and the public office of ministry. Perhaps the most convenient way to summarize their testimony is by pointing especially to the way they define certain terms.

Church for the reformers is always more event than organization and always encompasses in all times and places the assembly of believers around the events of Word and sacrament. In this church, there will always be the public office of ministry, which includes oversight, mutual accountability, and service to the assembled believers in the gospel.[15]

The *heart of the episcopal ministry* must always and only be ministry of Word and sacrament. The "to obtain such faith" of Articles 5 and 28 of the Augsburg Confession defines what all public ministers of the gospel do, regardless of their particular calling. Thus, the heart of episcopal ministry must be service (*ministerium*), not lordship. This ministry is transparent—that is, when it calls attention to itself as an end or goal in itself, it loses its authority because such claims undermine the very message of the gospel that it is called to serve. The authority of this office derives from the gospel, not from handing down authority from the laity to public ministers or from the succession of bishops to the ordained.

The *authority of bishops* is always determined by the two kinds of righteousness. With respect to this world and to ordering things in the churches, bishops have authority, regulated by their churches' constitutions (*de iure humano*). With respect to the gospel, bishops have the God-given right (*de iure divino*), by virtue of their office, to preach the gospel and to administer the sacraments and, one might add, to oversee the preaching of the gospel and administration of the sacraments by others.

Thus, for the sake of the church and the gospel that brings the church to life, *episcopal ministry especially involves oversight*. Indeed, there can be no public ministry without oversight. The fact that the Lutheran Confessions often mix together pastors and bishops represents not a denigration or elimination of the episcopal office of oversight, but a recognition that the ancient office of bishop rested in the head pastor of each town in the ancient church. The difference between pastor and bishop is a matter of calling. Pastors and bishops preside in churches—that is, they minister to (serve) the church with the gospel. From the earliest days of the Reformation, such oversight of the gospel involved oversight of teaching (carried out by the teachers of the church and some bishops) and oversight of clergy (carried out by bishops (*episkopoi*) and the Latin equivalent, *superintendentes*, and by some teachers). This oversight implied the examination of and ordination of candidates for the public office of ministry in the church.

The *functions of oversight* provided by evangelical bishops include making regulations for the church's good order, working for the church's visible unity, and encouraging the authorities of this world toward greater justice.

Regulations must serve the good order of the church and must themselves never be confused with salvation and must never ensnare consciences. The salvation and rescue of the church never rests in traditions or practices, all of which can and must change over time. Thus, bishops do not have a power to rule over the church but have only the authority to serve the gospel for the church. Apostolic authority, at all levels, must mean allowing people to hear Christ's word of forgiveness and reconciliation. In this regard, the multiplication of regulations in many churches must always be judged by the question: "To what end?" Serving good order always implies creating space for the gospel.

The evangelical Christian can only refuse participation in *ecumenical endeavors* in which participants are ruled by anti-Christian impulses, that is, by any and all who claim sole rule (tyranny) in the church, the final word on all doctrine, and divine authority. In the view of Lutheran confessional writings, *evangelical episkopé* (Greek for oversight) and *evangelical bishops* by definition cannot cause schism in the church; only the failure of church leaders to preach the gospel and to protect others who preach the gospel can cause such schism.

One part of the evangelical ministry of bishops may be to *encourage people in positions of governmental and societal authority* to exercise their authority in favor of justice for all. This political function is not expressly mentioned in the Augsburg Confession precisely because the document itself, especially as measured by the preface (and Article 16), is working in this way.

When determining the role of bishops in today's church, two questions must be asked: what does this have to do with the gospel, and, derivatively, what does this have to do with good order in the church? The gospel is the free forgiveness of sins in Jesus Christ that justifies the ungodly by God's unlimited mercy through faith alone. This gospel always brings comfort to the weak and terrified. When either the content or the effect of the gospel is not preserved, then the authority of the public office of ministry is also compromised. Thus, justifiable defiance of the authority of oversight in the church occurs *only* when the gospel itself is at stake. The only reason the reformers ever give for not following the episcopal ordering of the church of their day was when bishops raged against or became enemies of the gospel. The only reason for which one can reject the present order of the church, legitimate changes in such ordering, or the authority of anyone in a position of oversight is abandonment of the gospel itself. The only reasons for refusing to follow a particular church order must be of the most serious nature (eschatologically): idolatry, tyranny, and injustice.

We live in a world infected by the corporate sin of individualism, a particularly lethal form of idolatry. This cancer has invaded the church in insidious ways. No one will submit to anyone else. Individual congregations assert their power over clergy and curse the wider church. Individual members of the clergy assert their power over congregational members and curse the wider church. Individuals shop for the church that meets their needs and curse the wider church. Professors of theology are no exceptions. To bring the message of forgiveness and reconciliation, God instituted the office of public ministry; to maintain good order in the church and to oversee that preaching, we have bishops, exercising their God-given authority to preach the gospel through such oversight.[16] Now, to apply Luther's description of himself and other pastors to bishops, he or she will not look like much and will be little more than a *Madensack*—a bag of maggots, food for worms.[17] Yet God has chosen to work through such broken persons—a sign of the cross to spite the devil. Rather than arguing about whether to have bishops or how much power to give them or how they relate to the apostles, perhaps we should instead thank God for having revived, renewed, and reformed this great office of gospel service in Luther's day and in our own.

Concluding Thoughts

So, how far have we come in this historical excursion? Far enough, I hope, to cast doubt on some of American Lutheranism's most cherished ideas about the reformers' views on the common priesthood of the whole people of God. Far enough to realize that at heart the public office of ministry and its authority begins and ends with the proclamation of the free forgiveness of sin in Christ Jesus our Lord. Far enough to realize that oversight, far from being a curse imposed upon the church by the power-hungry, can and should be one of the church's richest assets for the weak and those who serve them.

First and foremost, the priesthood of all believers is not a scheme for giving power to the laity, nor is it an excuse for dividing up Christ's church or diminishing its public offices. When Luther says that we are all priests, bishops, and popes, it is one of his most poignant pleas for *unity* in the church, that is, for unity among the members of the body of Christ. To say "we are priests because we share Christ's priesthood in baptism" is the same as saying "through baptism we are the body of Christ." There are no loose cannons on the ship of the church; no single member of the body who can say, "Because you are not the hand, we have no need of you"; no single person who can arrogate to himself or herself the sacerdotal priesthood we share in Christ. There is only one *Stand*, one walk of life in the church.

Second, and equally important, there is a great variety of offices within the church. Perhaps the most important aspect of that variety is simply this: there are the offices of speaker and hearer, of celebrant and recipient, of baptizer and baptizand. There is the one who, in Christ's name and in his stead, forgives and the one who is forgiven. Now, in a public emergency which we must always define not as a matter of convenience but as a real, dial-911, call-in-the-fire-and-police-departments and, for that matter, send-in-the-Marines kind of emergency—in such a situation, when the public minister of the gospel is not available or is unwilling to fulfill his or her office, then anyone, by virtue of his or her inclusion in Christ's body and Christ's priesthood (that is, by virtue of his or her baptism), may step into this public office and exercise its authority (which is, do not forget, an authority of service in any case). Anyone must do this in an emergency because the Word and sacraments do not belong to any of us individually (whether we are called and ordained or not) but belong to Christ and through Christ, the High Priest, belong to his body of spiritual priests, that is, to the whole church. In fact, the whole church (all the baptized) participate in each and every sacrament. We cannot preach without hearers, baptize without the unbaptized, celebrate the Supper without thankful recipients, or forgive sins without someone there to receive forgiveness. Outside of such emergency, everyone should exercise his or her offices according to his or her gifts. Pastors need shoes; congregations need good administrators; all can share their wealth. Within the one body of Christ, there are places for all to serve.

Third, there is one office that Christ has set up in the church, the authority of which comes directly from him ("Whoever hears you, hears me"). It is the public office of ministry, the call to proclaim at the end of the world on the rooftops what we have heard and believed in secret. This office must be filled, because Christ insists that the Word get out. In the household, that public minister may be the father and mother; in the congregation, it is the pastor, preacher, teacher, or other servant ordered to do this work publicly; in the greater church, it is the pastor of a zip code or the bishop. When those placed into this special, public office refuse or simply fail to speak out, God raises up voices from the stones or from children or from the least and the weakest to fulfill this holy office in that emergency of silence.

The office is neither lording it over other Christians nor being a slave to other Christians' whims. The abuse of the public office of ministry is widespread and has resulted in no end of harm. But whether such abuse arises from delusions of grandeur or from catering to cultural fads and fancies, it always presupposes an abandonment of the very office itself, precisely because the office is one of service to the gospel. Such abuse, however, is not cured by abandoning the public ministry.

It is an office of service to the gospel for the sake of the body of Christ and the world. The public minister is, to use Paul's word in 2 Corinthians, an ambassador. The authority resides in the Word and thus in the office, not in the person. Thus, the person is transparent. One does not see the minister at the font, but rather sees Christ; one does not hear the preacher's words from the pulpit, but rather hears Christ's word; one is not received at the Table by the host pastor, for Christ is the host; and one certainly does not receive the pastor's body and blood, but receives Christ's. Indeed, at the Supper, the pastor comes closest to demonstrating by his or her actions precisely what the public office of ministry is all about: service at the Lord's Table.[1]

As an aside, this probably means that all of our complicated distinctions in today's church between "Word and sacrament" and "Word and service" ministries are rather misplaced, though perhaps inevitable as we seek decent ways to order our church's life. There is only service in the public office of ministry, and different people are called to exercise different aspects of this public ministry: baptizing, preaching, teaching, serving the poor, administering, praying, serving the Supper. Demands by diaconal ministers for some sort of ordination are completely contrary to their various callings to serve (and, thus, not to demand). Demands by pastors not to expand ordination to include those who serve in other ways than at Pulpit, Table, and Bath also strike a hollow chord. Demands to exclude bishops from ordination or consecration simply mistake their service for some sort of imaginary power a power that any bishop will confess does not exist in that office. The point must instead be to preach, teach, celebrate, consecrate, ordain, and, in short, serve up the gospel in big, delicious, faith-filling portions.

Frankly, we need to treat these public servants with more respect. For example, the mistreatment of pastors throughout the church is simply a travesty. Congregations and individual members seem to think that it is open season on any public servant of the gospel who does not do what he or she is told or who does not fulfill the needs of this or that individual. So many pastors have simply become cynical—witness the number who, when meeting a potential public minister (a seminarian, intern, ordinand, or even just someone who expresses an interest in becoming a pastor or rostered leader in the church), will make a joke demeaning the office or roll their eyes and warn the person about what is in store or—by far the most often—simply go to great lengths (often by silence) not to interest anyone in their calling.

Yet we ought to remember Luther's amazing comments in his booklet on Psalm 82. Here, in urging his prince and others in authority to support pastors, he described that office in this way:

> Many kings and princes have founded great, glorious churches and built temples . . . but how would all of these large, glorious things compare to a right, honest, God-fearing pastor or preacher? Such a one can help thousands of souls both for eternal life and in this life. For he can bring them to God through the Word and make them into productive, capable people, who serve and honor God and, at the same time, are beneficial and useful in the world. . . . But [compared with glittering church buildings] who is a pastor? And who has eyes to see such a virtue in a lord or prince? Supporting or protecting a poor, honest pastor or preacher does not shine or sparkle; it is really nothing at all to look at. But to build a marble church or give golden jewels, to serve dead stone and wood, now that sparkles, that shines, that is called a royal, princely virtue! Well, let it shine and let it sparkle, while my dingy pastor practices the virtue that increases God's realm, fills heaven with saints, plunders

hell, robs the devil, protects from death, restrains sin and, moreover, instructs and comforts the world—each in his or her own walk of life—supports peace and unity, trains fine young people and plants all kinds of virtues in the people. In short, he creates a new world and builds not a temporary, pitiable house but an eternal, beautiful paradise, in which God himself wants to dwell.[2]

To be sure, there are countless pastors and congregational members who know what a difference it makes to have someone, in the person and stead of Christ and with the blessing of the whole church, to stand by the bedside and at the graveside, to offer faithful expositions of God's word that proclaim judgment and hope, to defend the poor, to teach the ignorant (and, yes, even hormonally challenged eighth graders), to encourage the fainthearted, and to celebrate the Supper and baptize. But how easy it is to forget what this calling is all about and to denigrate the amazing ministry of that one remarkable hour on the Lord's Resurrection Day and of all the hours culminating in and leading away from that hour!

Fourth, we need bishops, people whose public calling it is to exercise oversight among us. Actually, we need three kinds of bishops. We need *bishops in the household* who understand and exercise their callings as Christian parents (and, in some situations, surrogate parents) to teach and instruct God's dear children in the wonders of their baptisms. This means teaching the catechism— not as dry words out of a book, but first, as the baptizing word that daily drowns (that is the word of law, aptly summarized in the Ten Commandments) and raises up to new life (that is, the word of gospel, aptly summarized in the Creed), and second, as a word that cries to God for the baptizing grace only God can give (that is, the word of prayer, aptly summarized in the Our Father), and third, as a word about baptism and the Supper that gather us to assemble with other Christians.

We also need *bishops of the zip code*: pastors and other leaders who look at their parish as their ministry (to use an old expression) and at the people within their zip code as the ones they serve. The oversight in each zip code, exercised in cooperation and collaboration with other servants of the gospel, means that each pastor takes responsibility to see that the people are being fed with God's word and sacraments, that the lost and straying sheep are found, that younger and elder brothers (and sisters) are invited to the Father's feast, that the Word gets shouted from the rooftops. But such oversight also demands real care for those who are broken and hurting. It means providing care for those in hospitals and nursing homes, providing protection for "the other" (those of other language, race, religion—the list is endless) in our midst, especially for the Lazarus at our gates.

Finally, we need *bishops* (and teachers, it turns out) *in the wider church*, in our synods and denominations. They exercise oversight of congregations and pastors alike, of those who are under their care and for whom they care by serving. A bishop once told me that, when he visited a congregation whose pastor had just resigned his or her call, he would remind the congregation that they had two pastors (that is, two servants!) and that it was his office as bishop to see that the Word and sacraments were administered in this congregation until they could call another (second!) pastor. That responsibility for all those vacant parishes is no small matter.

Then there are all of those fires in all of those congregations in which there has been dysfunction or abuse or a breakdown between leaders and congregants. More often than not, it is the bishop and his or her staff who are called upon to make peace, to bring healing, and (sometimes) to raise the dead. What puzzles me is why, when few if any people object to bishops functioning in such crises, we do not more freely give these servants the added joy and honor of presiding at ordinations, where, by their very laying on of hands, they, on behalf of the whole church in all times and places, are taking responsibility for the ministry of that person. Since both Luther and Melanchthon *expected* evangelical bishops, in those few instances when there were such bishops, and superintendents to ordain, how can we who have an entire church filled with gospel-centered bishops allow for any less?

Ordination has to do with providing public ministers of the gospel for the church. It has to do with the gospel, of which bishops, too, are servants on behalf of Christ for the whole church. We need, desperately need, men and women in the church who will exercise the service of oversight in the gospel. As with bishops of the household or the zip code, these bishops have at heart service to the gospel. They bleed with every closed or failed congregation; they rejoice with every new ministry and healthy parish. For them, it has to do with overseeing preaching and teaching the gospel and celebrating the sacraments in every corner of that synod; it means overseeing candidates for ministry; and it means special care for the greater visible unity of Christ's church and for the poor and forgotten at our doors. This is no office of power; it is, once again, a ministry, a service, a laying down of one's life for Christ's sake and for the gospel. Even though our imperfect processes, whatever they have been throughout the church's history, rarely if ever will find for this office people who are conformed to the gospel or have the mind of Christ, this office of oversight does a great job of trans-forming and re-minding people and making them into good servant overseers.

In each of these four things—one spiritual priesthood in Christ, many callings among us, the public office of ministry, and offices of oversight—the most important thing is the word of God, that precious "good news of a great joy that shall be to all the people." Despite having produced this little book on the subject of the public ministry, we must remember that, for Lutherans, this ministry and its ordering are always secondary subjects when compared to the angel's message to the shepherds. One striking depiction of this in the sixteenth century comes down to us in the front pages of two very different Bibles of the time. In reaction to Luther's 1522 New Testament, Luther's bitter enemy George, the Duke of Saxony, had his court theologian produce a "Roman-friendly" version (basically, Luther's translation with different marginal notes and introductions). The frontispiece, created especially for this work, depicted the Father and the Holy Spirit with Jesus saying to Peter and Paul (the patron saints of the Roman pope), "Whoever hears you hears me." By contrast, the first printing of Wittenberg's complete Bible, released in 1534, shows the distinction between law and gospel. On the left side, the artist, Lukas Cranach, depicts Christ coming in judgment, the plague of vipers among the Israelites, the fall into sin of Adam and Eve and, at the bottom, this "Old Adam" being driven into hell by the devil, death, and the law, personified by Moses holding the two tablets of the Ten Commandments. The other half of this illustration, divided by a tree that is withered on the law side and blooming on the gospel side, shows first Christ's ascension, the incarnation (where a baby holding a cross is coming to Mary, the second Eve), the announcement to the shepherds, the Resurrection (Christ victoriously slaying death and the devil in front of an empty tomb), and Christ on the cross, at the base of which stands John the Baptist pointing the "New Adam" (onto whom Christ's blood is streaming) to the "Lamb of God who takes away the sin of the world." That is, rather than worrying so much about who has authority to preach and teach, these early Lutherans concentrated instead on the message itself: the law that kills and the gospel that gives life (2 Corinthians 3:6). Indeed, one favorite way of depicting Luther in this period was to show him as John the Baptist pointing to Christ, the Lamb of God.

There may be better or worse ways to order ministry or even to make ecumenical agreements, but they finally must bend not simply to their calling (to be servant messengers) but to the message itself. "To you . . . is born a savior!" "Behold, the Lamb of God!" For finally, "in the end," everything hangs from the cross of the resurrected one. There is no one else to whom we may turn except to him. There is no one whom we serve except him. There is, truly, no other gospel.

Notes

Preface

1. First published as "The Priesthood of All Believers and Other Pious Myths," in *Saying and Doing the Gospel Today*, ed. Rhoda Schuler, Occasional Papers of the Institute of Liturgical Studies, no. 12 (Valparaiso, Ind.: Institute of Liturgical Studies, 2007), 92–115.

1. The Priesthood of All Believers and Other Pious Myths

1. The closest is in WA 8:254, 7 (LW 39:237), where Luther refers to "*das eynige gemeyne priesterthum*" (the one common priesthood).

2. That is, "*die Auffrichtung und fleissige übung deß Geistlichen Priesterthums*" (the establishment and diligent exercise of the spiritual priesthood). Cited in *TRE* 27:406.

3. *TRE* 27:402–10.

4. "Erneuerung der Verkündigung des allgemeinen Priestertums aus *Speners* Herz und Mund." For a very thoughtful refutation of the connection between Luther and Spener, one that calls into question Luther's "invention" of the priesthood of all believers, see Norman Nagel, "Luther and the Priesthood of All Believers," *Concordia Theological Quarterly* 61 (1997): 277–98, especially 295. He also realizes that there is little difference between the arguments of the Roman sacerdotalists and the later Pietists.

5. See his *Commentarius super priorem D. Petri Epistolam, in quo textus declaratur, quaestiones dubiae solvuntur, observationes eruuntur & loca in speciem pugnantia conciliantur* (Jena: Lobenstein, 1641) on 1 Peter 2:8.

6. Georg Rietschel, *Luther und die Ordination* (Wittenberg: R. Herrosé, 1883), especially 30–42, where he claims that the most important result of the doctrine of justification is the priesthood of all believers. A second edition of this volume was published in 1889.

7. Rietschel, *Luther und die Ordination*, 102ff. "Vielmehr ist die Einzelgemeinde schon Kirche,weil in ihr alle wesentlichen Momente der Kirche, die Gemeinschaft der Gläubigen, in der Wort und Sacrament

verwaltet wird, zum vollgültigen Ausdruck kommt." (Much more is the individual congregation already church, because in it all the essential ingredients of the church, the community of believers, administered in Word and Sacrament, come to full expression.) See Theodor Kliefoth, *Liturgische Abhandlungen* (Schwerin and Rostock: Stiller, 1854).

8. Friedrich Stahl, *Die Kirchenverfassung nach Lehre und Recht der Protestanten*, 2nd ed. (Erlangen: Bläsing, 1862 [1st ed.: 1840]), 394ff.; and Johann Höfling, *Grundsätze evangelisch-lutherischer Kirchenverfassung*, 3rd ed. (Erlangen: Bläsing, 1853). For a history of this earlier debate, involving particularly Friedrich Stahl and Johann Höfling in the mid-nineteenth century, see Harald Goertz, *Allgemeines Priestertum und ordiniertes Amt bei Luther* (Marburg: N. G. Elwert, 1997), 1–27.

9. Rietschel, *Luther und die Ordination*, 42: "Nicht ist für [Luther] ein besonderes Amt der Institution seitens Christo für das Predigtamt nötig, es ist vielmehr mit dem vollbrachten heil für die geordnete Gemeinde dadurch von selbst gegeben."

10. Rietschel, *Luther und die Ordination*, 112: "Rechte Pastoren sind wir nur dann, wenn und soweit als wir lebendige Christen sind." (We are only then true pastors if and insofar as we we living Christians.)

11. See Goertz, *Allgemeines Priestertum.*

12. These include Cyril Eastwood, *The Priesthood of All Believers* (Minneapolis: Augsburg, 1962); Roy A. Harrisville, *Ministry in Crisis: Changing Perspectives on Ordination and the Priesthood of All Believers* (Minneapolis: Augsburg, 1987); Herschel H. Hobbs, *You Are Chosen: The Priesthood of All Believers* (San Francisco: Harper & Row, 1990); and Carl R. Trueman, "Reformers, Puritans and Evangelicals: The Lay Connection," in *The Rise of the Laity in Evangelical Protestantism*, ed. Deryck W. Lovegrove (London: Routledge, 2002), 17–35.

13. See WA 38:401–11. A more recent and thorough study of this problem, which could not be fully integrated into this study, is Martin Krarup, *Ordination in Wittenberg: Die Einsetzung in das kirchliche Amt in Kursachsen zur Zeit der Reformation* (Tübingen: Mohr Siebeck, 2007). See my forthcoming review in http://www.h-net.org/reviews.

14. See "The Augsburg Confession, V," trans. Eric Gritsch, in *The Book of Concord*, ed. Robert Kolb and Timothy J. Wengert (Minneapolis: Fortress Press, 2000).

15. Tappert's position is echoed four years later in a tract by Erwin Mülhaupt, *Allgemeines Priestertum oder Klerikalismus?* (Stuttgart: Calwer,

1963). In the foreword (p. 5ff.), he champions the priesthood of all believers against any and all Romanizing and ecumenical tendencies! As an example of his idiosyncratic reading of Luther, see comments on *Daß eine christliche Versammlung oder Gemeine Recht und Macht habe, alle Lehre zu urteilen und Lehrer zu berufen, ein- und abzusetzen, Grund und Ursach aus der Schrift* (1523; WA 11:408–16 [LW 39:301–14]). "Man könnte diese Schrift den Freiheitsbrief und die Magna Charta der christlichen Gemeinde nennen, die Freiheit, Recht und Vollmacht der christlichen Gemeinde auf das allgemeine Priestertum der Gläubigen begründet." (One could call this tract the declaration of independence and the Magna Carta of the Christian congregation, because it grounds the freedom, right and complete authority of the Christian congregation upon the common priesthood of all believers.) Not only is that *not* what this tract is about, it also completely misconstrues Luther's theology by ignoring the historical context of the tract.

16. Even Mülhaupt's tendentious tract admits that Luther did not see the concept of the priesthood of all believers as undercutting the ministerial office. Unfortunately, Mülhaupt (ibid., 17–19), like many others, describes the pastoral office as deriving its authority from the priesthood of all believers.

17. WA 6:381–469 (LW 44:115–217). For the dating, see WA 6:392.

18. WA 6:352–78 (LW 35:75–111).

19. WA Br 1:595, 26–42.

20. WA 7:20-38 (LW 31:327–77); WA 6:497–573 (LW 36:3–126); WA 7:308–457; WA 12:160–96 (LW 40:3–44); WA 38:195–256; WA 41:79–239 (LW 13:225–348).

21. See Heiko Oberman, *Luther: Man between God and the Devil* (New Haven, Conn.: Yale University Press, 1989), 40–49.

22. WA 6:407, 10–12 (LW 44:127). Here and throughout, translations are by the author.

23. WA 6:407, 13–19 (LW 44:127).

24. For a description of the origins of this battle over *Übertragungslehre* versus *Stiftungstheorie* in the nineteenth century, see Goertz, *Allgemeines Priestertum*, 1–27, and *TRE* 27:405. Unfortunately, the authors of the *TRE* article (Goertz and Wilfried Härle, his *Doktorvater*) finally come out in favor of a kind of functional definition of the ordained ministry, in part by misconstruing sixteenth-century understandings of

the words *Amt* and *Stand* (e.g., "Nirgends proklamiert Luther jedoch ein besonderes göttliches Gebot für die Institution des ordinierten Amtes" [Nowhere does Luther ever proclaim a divine command for the institution of the ordained office] and "Die zahlreiche Stiftungsaussagen bei Luther beziehen sich nicht auf das [ordinierte] Amt, sondern auf den [Pfarr-] Stand" [The countless statements establishing it in Luther relate not to the (ordained) office but to the pastoral estate]). Thus, they still derive the authority of the pastoral office from the priesthood of all believers. Had it ever occurred to them that the priesthood of all believers itself was a later construct of Pietists, and not of Luther, they might have avoided this dichotomy.

25. For one use of this term, see Klaus Petzold, *Die Grundlagen der Erziehungslehre im Spätmittelalter und bei Luther* (Heidelberg: Quelle & Meyer, 1969).

26. Timothy J. Wengert, "'Peace, Peace . . . Cross, Cross': Reflections on How Martin Luther Relates the Theology of the Cross to Suffering," *Theology Today* 59 (2002): 190–205.

27. Here Harald Goertz, "Allgemeines Priestertum," *RGG⁴*, 1:317, is correct in saying, "Da das 'Priestersein' eine (bildhafte) Umschreibung für das Christsein ist, kann es auch nicht anders *begründet* sein als dieses, nämlich im Rechtfertigungsgeschehen." (Since "being priest" is a [pictorial] paraphrase of "being Christian," it cannot be established in any other way than in the event of justification.) *TRE* 27:404 lists other instances where Luther equated priesthood with being Christian. See, especially, WA 10/3:308ff. (a sermon delivered on the twelfth Sunday after Trinity, 1522) and 12:318, 18–21 (a 1522 sermon on 1 Peter 2:18 [LW 30:64]).

28. WA 6:407, 19–25 (LW 44:127).

29. See the discussion by Harald Goertze and Wilfried Härle in *TRE* 27:402–10. They stress the metaphoric use of the term by Luther (and use the more accurate "Priestersein" [priestly existence] rather than "Priestertum" [priesthood]) and point out that Luther had to redefine the ordained office at the same time.

30. WA 6:407, 29—408, 2 (LW 44:128).

31. WA 6:408, 2–7 (LW 44:128).

32. See the "Treatise on the Power and Primacy of the Pope," 67, trans. Jane Strohl, in *The Book of Concord*, ed. Robert Kolb and Timothy J. Wengert (Minneapolis: Fortress Press, 2000), 341. The citation is

from Gratian, *Decretum* III, dist. 4, ch. 36, citing a supposed letter from Augustine to Fortunatus.

33. For a look at how this played out in Luther's later controversies with lawyers, see the forthcoming article by James Estes in *Luther-Jahrbuch*. There Luther drew the line at the conscience.

34. WA 6:408, 11–21 (LW 44:129).

35. This is the most important contribution of Goertz's work (*Allgemeines Preistertum*, 33–79).

36. For another, clearly metaphorical use of the notion that all Christians are priests, see Luther's *Freedom of a Christian* (WA 7:26–29 [LW 31:353–56]).

37. WA 6:408, 15–17 (LW 44:129).

38. Of course, Luther's use of this term *Stand* varied, so that in other settings he could talk about three *Stände* (estates, or walks of life) in which one exercises various offices.

39. WA 6:408, 26–35 (LW 44:129–30).

40. WA 6:409, 5–10 (LW 44:130).

41. WA 6:409, 22–25 (LW 44:131).

42. This is the kernel of his arguments against the papacy spelled out in more detail in *The Freedom of a Christian* and the accompanying letter to Pope Leo X. For a striking interpretation of these two documents, see Berndt Hamm, "Luther's *Freedom of a Christian* and the Pope," *Lutheran Quarterly* 20 (2007): 249–67.

2. Other "Proofs" for the Existence of the Priesthood of All Believers

1. *Ein Sermon von dem neuen Testament, das ist von der heiligen Messe*, 1520 (WA 6:349–78 [LW 35:75–111]).

2. WA 6:370, 7–11 (LW 35:100–101). See also Luther's lengthy discussion of this issue in *Vom Mißbrauch der Messe* (1521), WA 8:486–90; 486, 27–28: "Diß ist eyn geystlich priesterthum, allen Christen gemeyn, da durch wyr alle mit Christo priester sind, das ist, wyr sind kinder Christi, des hochsten preisters." (This is a spiritual priesthood, held by all Christians in common, through which we are all priests with Christ, that is, we are all children of Christ, the High Priest.) For Luther, to be a priest is to be Christ's children, not power-hungry parishioners or pastors.

3. This is one of the places where Harald Goertz, *Allgemeines Priestertum und ordiniertes Amt bei Luther* (Marburg: N. G. Elwert,

1997), 155ff. and 184ff., is most confused. By extracting Luther's comments from their original context, Goertz blithely applies this text and others to his theory that the ordained priesthood derives its authority from the priesthood of all believers.

4. WA 6:370, 16–32.

5. The word *instituendis* is a gerund for a word that is sometimes used by Luther as the equivalent of "ordained," or (literally) "to put in place."

6. For a brief analysis of this tract, see Reinhard Schwarz, "Geistliche Vollmacht: Luther über allgemeines Priestertum und kirchliches Amt (1523)," *Luther* 77 (2006): 74–82. Schwarz rightly stresses the spiritual nature of the common priesthood and rejects any notions that derive the authority of the public ministry from this priesthood. Thus, although he concludes (p. 81ff.), "The public office itself is not subject to the will of the congregation," he goes on to add: "Much more the Word of God demands its public dissemination that in a particular emergency situation an individual Christian is justified in exercising the full authority of the common priesthood without having been given responsibility for it by the congregation." I would only argue that in such a situation, the individual is not so much exercising the full authority of the common priesthood as he or she is exercising the full authority of the public office. See below and chapter 1.

7. WA 12:171, 17—172, 8 (LW 40:9), here 171, 17–23: "It would be safer and more salutary, were the paterfamilias to read the gospel to his household and to baptize (since the consensus and usage of the entire world also permits this to the laity) those who are born and so to rule himself and his own in accord with the teaching of Christ, even if they dared not or could not receive the Eucharist their whole life long. For in a crisis the Eucharist is not necessary for salvation, but the Gospel and Baptism suffice, since faith alone justifies and Charity alone lives well." Goertz, *Allgemeines Priestertum*, 155ff., misses this point completely.

8. WA 12:171, 24–32 (LW 40:9–10): "Surely, if two, three, or ten households or a whole city or many cities agreed among themselves and practiced faith and charity through the domestic Gospel, although no ordained, tonsured or anointed person or a minister who was by some means imposed [on them] who would administer the Eucharist or other things ever came among them, Christ would without a doubt be in their midst and acknowledge them for his Church, and not only would

not condemn them but would plainly crown this pious and Christian abstinence from all other sacraments, administered by the ungodly and sacrilegious. For he himself said (Luke 10:42) that one thing alone is necessary, namely the Word of God in which a person lives."

9. WA 12:172, 35—173, 7 (LW 40:11): "Nam cum ista ordinatio autoritate scripturarum, deinde exemplo et decretis Apostolorum in hoc sit instituta, ut ministros verbi in populo institueret: Ministerium publicum inquam verbi, quo dispensantur mysteria dei, per sacram ordinationem institui debet, ceu res, quae omnium in Ecclesia et summa et maxima est, in qua tota vis Ecclesiastici status consistit, cum sine verbo nihil constet in Ecclesia et per solum verbum omnia constent. Papistae autem mei de hoc ministerio ne somniant quidem in suis ordinibus." (Here and elsewhere, the translations are those of the author.)

10. WA 12:178, 9–10 (LW 40:18): "SACERDOTEM NON ESSE QUOD PRESBYTERUM VEL ministrum, illum nasci, hunc fieri."

11. WA 12:179, 38–40 (LW 40:21). "Sed pergamus et idem ex officiis sacerdotalibus (quae vocant) probemus, omnes Christianos ex aequo esse sacerdotes. Nam illud 1. Petri 2[:9]: 'Vos estis regale sacerdotium', et Apoca. 5[:10]: 'Fecisti nos deo regnum et sacerdotes.'"

12. WA 12:178, 21–33 (LW 40:19): "First, let this therefore stand as that unbreakable rock. In the New Testament there is not and cannot be a sacerdotal priest externally anointed. Whoever are so anointed are frauds and idols, because there is neither example nor prescription nor any word of this their vanity in the Gospels or the Apostolic epistles, but having been falsely invented by human beings, in the same way that Jeroboam did in Israel, they have been erected and introduced. For a sacerdotal priest particularly in the New Testament is not made but born, is not ordained by created. But it is born by the birth not of the flesh but of the Spirit, namely from water and the Spirit (John 3) in the bath of regeneration (Titus). And in short all Christians are sacerdotal priests and all sacerdotal priests are Christians. For it is asserted outside the Word of God, only from the dictates of human beings or ancient usage or the multitude of opinions of which whatever stands for an article of faith is sacrilege and abomination, as I have said elsewhere at length."

13. WA 12:178, 37—179, 5 (LW 40:19): "Christus enim neque rasus neque oleo unctus est, ut sacerdos fieret. Quare nec ulli Christum sequenti ungi satis est, ut sacerdos fiat, sed longe aliud habeat necesse est,

quod cum habuerit, oleo et rasura opus non habet. Ut videas Episcopos larvarum ordinatores sacrilege errare, dum suas uncturas et ordinationes sic necessarias faciunt, ut sine iis sacerdotem fieri negent, etiam si sit sanctissimus, vel Christus ipse." Thus, if there is any place for a doctrine of transference, it would be here: that baptism transfers all Christians into Christ's priesthood so that they share in the benefits of his work and office.

14. WA 12:180, 2–4 (LW 40:21).

15. WA 12:180, 18 (LW 40:21).

16. WA 12:182, 19–27 (LW 40:24): "Tercium officium est consecrare seu ministrare sacrum panem et vinum. Hic vero triumphant ac regnant Rasorum ordines, hanc potestatem neque angelis neque matri virgini concedunt. Sed missis illorum insaniis dicimus et hoc officium esse omnibus commune, perinde atque sacerdotium, idque non nostra, sed Christi asserimus autoritate, dicentis in coena novissima: 'Hoc facite in meam commemorationem', quo verbo etiam rasi papistae volunt sacerdotes factos et potentiam consecrandi collatam. At hoc verbum dixit Christus omnibus suis praesentibus et futuris, qui panem illum ederent et poculum biberent. Quicquid ergo ibi collatum est, omnibus collatum est."

17. WA 12:180, 24–32 (LW 40:21–22). The WA refers to Jerome Emser and to Luther's tracts against him. See, especially, *Ein Widerspruch D. Luthers seines Irrthums, erzwungen durch den allerhochgelehrtesten Priester Gottes, Hernn Hieronymo Emser, Vicarien zu Meißen*, 1521–22 (WA 8:250, 20–26 [LW 39:233]): "Ich Martin Luther bekenn, das ich eyntrechtlich mitt dem hochgelerten herrn und gottis priester, Herr Hierony. Emser, hallte und stymme, das der spruch S. Petri nit alleyn von der geystlichen, ßondern auch von der leyplichen, odder, das ichs auffs klerlichst sag, von aller priesterschafft, die in der Christenheit ist, zuvorstehen sey: das rede ich auß gantzem ernst. Denn ich hab yn der warheit zuvor die sach nit recht angesehen. Nu hoff ich, Luter sey nit mehr ein ketzer, und hab mich mit Emsern gar voreynigt." (I, Martin Luther, confess, that in complete agreement with the highly educated man and priest of God, Mr. Jerome Emser, I hold and insist that the saying of St. Peter is to be understood not only concerning the spiritual but also concerning the bodily priesthood. Or, that I may say it most clearly, it applies to every priesthood that there is in Christendom. This I say in all seriousness, for I did not in truth rightly perceive the thing

before this. Now I hope that Luther is no longer a heretic and that I am in complete agreement with Emser.)

18. WA 12:189, 17–27 (LW 40:34): "Verum haec omnia de iure communi Christianorum diximus. Nam cum omnium Christianorum haec sint omnia (uti probavimus) communia, nulli licet in medium prodire autoritate propria et sibi arripere soli, quod omnium est. Arripe sane id iuris et exequere, ubi nullus est, qui simile ius habeat. Verum haec communio iuris cogit, ut unus, aut quotquot placuerint communitati, eligantur vel acceptentur, qui vice et nomine omnium, qui idem iuris habent, exequantur officia ista publice, ne turpis sit confusio in populo dei, et Babylon quaedam fiat in Ecclesia, sed omnia secundum ordinem fiant, ut Apostolus docuit. Aliud enim est ius publice exequi, aliud iure in necessitate uti: publice exequi non licet, nisi consensu universitatis seu Ecclesiae. In necessitate utatur quicunque voluerit." Goertz and Härle, in their article in *TRE* 27:404, misconstrue Luther's earlier use of 1 Corinthians 14:26 (WA 12:181, 11–22 [LW 40:22–23]) by assuming that he was arguing in favor of an individualized appropriation of this common priesthood. However, *as Luther's own words indicate*, he was proving that Paul's words did not apply just to "the tonsured," as he called them. "Dic ergo, quid est 'unusquisque'? Quid est 'omnes'? an Rasos solos haec communi voce signat? . . . Quare et sacerdotium non nisi unicum et omnibus commune, qui Christiani sunt, non modo iure, sed et praecepto." (Tell me, what is "each"? What is "all"? Is Paul designating only the tonsured with this common word? . . . Therefore the priesthood is nothing except a unity and common to all who are Christians, not simply by right but by command.)

19. WA 12:189, 40—190, 6 (LW 40:34–35): "Nos in hoc stamus: Non esse aliud verbum dei, quam quod omnibus Christianis annunciari praecipitur. Non esse alium baptismum, quam quem quilibet Christanus conferre potest. Non esse aliam memoriam coenae dominicae, quam ubi quilibet Christianus facere potest, quod Christus facere instituit. Non esse aliud peccatum, quam quod Christianus quilibet ligare et solvere debet. Non esse aliud sacrificium, quam corpus cuiuslibet Christiani. Non posse orare nisi solum Christianum. Non debere iudicare de doctrinis nisi Christianum. Haec autem sunt sacerdotalia et regalia." On the Lord's Supper, it is important to remember that Christ instituted a "remembrance" involving both the one presiding and the ones receiving.

20. See, especially, WA 12:190, 11–23 (LW 40:35), where he listed the appropriate names for the public minister of the gospel (e.g., *Ministri, diaconi, Episcopi,* and *dispensatores*).

21. WA 12:192, 34—193, 8 (LW 40:39): "'Nova res est (inquiunt) et sine exemplo, sic eligere et creare Episcopos.' Respondeo: imo antiquissima et exemplis Apostolorum suorumque discipulorum probata, licet per papistas contrario exemplo et pestilentibus doctrinis abolita et extincta. Proinde hoc magis laborandum, ut recens pestilentiae exemplum explodatis et priscum salutis exemplum revocetis. Deinde, si maxime nova res esset, tamen cum verbum dei hic luceat et iubeat, simul necessitas animarum cogit, prorsus nihil movere debet rei novitas, sed verbi maiestas. Nam quid rogo non est novum, quod fides facit? Non fuit etiam Apostolorum tempore novum huiusmodi ministerium? Non fuit novum, quod Abraham obtulit filium suum? Non fuit novum, quod filii Israel mare transierunt? Non erit mihi novum, quod ego per mortem ibo in vitam? At verbum dei in his omnibus spectatur, non novitas ipsa, alioqui si novitas satis est ut moretur, iam non licet ulli verbo dei unquam credere."

22. WA 12:193, 22—194, 3 (LW 40:40).

23. *Von den Konziliis und Kirchen* (WA 50:509–653 [LW 41:3–178]).

24. WA 50:489: "Konzil und Kirche bedingen sich gegenseitig; beide haben sie ihr Wesen im allgemeinen Priestertum der Gläubigen, beiden gibt Leben und Grund die heilige Schrift." (Council and church are mutually dependent upon one another; both have their essence in the common priesthood of believers, and the Holy Scripture gives life and basis to both.)

25. WA 50:489: "[W]ährend Luther in unserer Schrift alles auf die grundlegende Bedeutung der heiligen Schrift zurückführt, er dort von dem Wesen der Kirche, dem allgemeinen Priestertum der Gläubigen den Ausgang nimmt." (Because Luther in this document traces everything back to the basic meaning of Holy Scripture, he takes his beginning point from the essence of the church, namely, the common priesthood of believers.)

26. WA 50:624–25 (LW 41:143–48). See also Gordon Lathrop and Timothy J. Wengert, *Christian Assembly: Marks of the Church in a Pluralistic Age* (Minneapolis: Fortress Press, 2004).

27. See Lathrop and Wengert, *Christian Assembly*, 39–43.

28. This notion of the continuity of Luther's thought is also one of Goertz's conclusions in *Allgemeines Priestertum*, 30 (where those holding the opposing viewpoints are listed), although he arrives at this conclusion without investigating whether the priesthood of all believers was ever a category of Luther's thought. At the same time, Martin Krarup, *Ordination in Wittenberg* (Tübingen: Mohr Siebeck, 2006), 15–18, is also correct in arguing for a change in Luther's understanding of ordination.

29. WA 50:632, 36—633, 5 (LW 41:154).

30. WA 50:633, 5–11 (LW 41:154): "For the general populace cannot do this but must entrust it to someone or let it be entrusted. Otherwise, what would happen if each wanted to speak or distribute, and no one would yield to the other. It has to be entrusted to one person alone, and that one must be allowed to preach, baptize, absolve, and distribute the sacrament. All the others must be satisfied and allow this to happen. Where you see this happening, then it is certain that God's people and the holy, Christian people are there."

31. WA 50:633, 12–24 (LW 41:154–55).

32. He argued for exclusion on the basis of Scripture and natural law.

33. WA 50:633, 25—634, 10 (LW 41:155).

34. WA 50:634, 34—641, 16 (LW 41:156–63).

35. WA 50:641, 16–19 (LW 41:164). Here he used the word *priest* in its (for his time) traditional sense of "public minister of the gospel."

36. Apology of the Augsburg Confession, 7/828, trans. Charles Arand, in *The Book of Concord*, ed. Robert Kolb and Timothy J. Wengert (Minneapolis: Fortress Press, 2000), 178.

3. The End of the Public Office of Ministry in the Lutheran Confessions

1. CA 4.1–3, trans. Eric Gritsch, in *BC 2000*, 38–41.

2. CA 4.1–3, German, in *BC 2000*, 38 and 40.

3. "The office of preaching" (CA 5.1 [German], in *BC 2000*, 40). This word embraces preaching, teaching, and administering the sacraments, as the modifying phrase ("giving the gospel and the sacraments") indicates. See below for a fuller discussion of this article.

4. CA 5.1–4, in *BC 2000*, 40.

5. The mention of the Anabaptists in CA 5 is actually secondary to the real opponent ("and others"), namely, such late-medieval scholastic

theologians as Gabriel Biel, who argued that the justified merited God's grace by exercising natural human powers, and Erasmus of Rotterdam, who opposed Luther in a debate over the freedom of the will. Luther pointed out a similar connection between contempt for the means of grace, justification, and ministry in the SA, trans. William Russell, 3.8.3–13, in *BC 2000*, 322–23. As Robert Kolb has suggested to me, CA 5 marks a dividing line between a religion that envisions God as reached by ritual and one that hears the God who speaks and enters into conversation with humanity.

6. SC, the Lord's Prayer, trans. Timothy J. Wengert, in *BC 2000*, 356–57.

7. SA 2, in *BC 2000*, 300. See especially SA 3.4.3–4, 10, in *BC 2000*, 307, 309. The citation of Revelation 10:3 and the use of the term *Endchrist* (end times Antichrist) here are no accident. For the development of Luther's understanding of the papacy, see Scott Hendrix, *Luther and the Papacy* (Philadelphia: Fortress Press, 1981).

8. SA 2.4.9.

9. TPPP 37, trans. Jane Strohl, in *BC 2000*, 336.

10. TPPP 39, in *BC 2000*, 337.

11. CA (German) 20.15, in *BC 2000*, 54. The Latin version (CA 20.17, in *BC 2000*, 55) is even stronger: "This whole teaching [about justification by faith alone] must be referred to that struggle of the terrified conscience, and it cannot be understood apart from that struggle."

12. Martin Luther, *Concerning the Ministry* (1523), trans. Conrad Bergendoff, in LW 40:25. As we saw in chapter 2, people have misconstrued Luther's remarks as deriving the authority of the office from the baptized or the priesthood of all believers. In fact, throughout his life, Luther held that the authority of the public office comes from Christ to the apostles and their successors (pastors and bishops) through the Word. Thus, he was not arguing simply that "everyone is baptized, so anyone can do this," but rather that the emergency authorizes any Christian to fulfill this public office. Thus, Luther did not imagine that sex or age was ever a barrier to fulfilling this public office of ministry in an emergency.

13. For a fuller use of this metaphor, see Gerhard O. Forde, "The Ordained Ministry," in *Called and Ordained: Lutheran Perspectives on the Office of the Ministry*, ed. Todd Nichol and Marc Kolden (Minneapolis: Fortress Press, 1990), 117–36, esp. 133. The reference to a child

forgiving sin comes from WA 49:312 (see Gordon Lathrop and Timothy J. Wengert, *Christian Assembly: Marks of the Church in a Pluralistic Age* [Minneapolis: Fortress Press, 2004], 155).

14. *Sermon on Good Works*, WA 6:250–65 [LW 44:80–100]; *Confession* of 1528, WA 26:504–5 [LW 37:364–65].

15. *Die Doppelschichtigkeit in Luthers Kirchenbegriff* (Gotha: Klotz, 1928), 117ff. This was originally published as "Die Doppelschichtigkeit in Luthers Kirchenbegriff," *Theologische Studien und Kritiken* 100 (1928): 197–347. Kattenbusch's work is laced with the presuppositions of Ritschlian liberalism and idealism. Moreover, he accepts without serious reflection Pietism's division between laity and clergy. Thus, on page 120 (emphasis in the original), he writes, "The laity is *of itself* responsible for its actions in their calling as Christians thus also for their calling in the church." Moreover, the entire section (pp. 117–49) contains no references to the *Predigtamt* whatsoever but only a very confused discussion of the three hierarchies in Luther's thought. This means that the BSLK gives no textual or scholarly arguments whatsoever for its comment, the origins of which may be sought in the confusion after the end of Protestant hegemony in the Prussian-German state following the imperial abdication of 1918.

16. See chapter 1.

17. The fact that Luther occasionally used the term to describe the official functions of the father or mother in the household indicates a metaphorical use of the term (he also calls parents bishops and bishopesses). Here it must be noted that the housefather and housemother (and the household) were public offices both in Luther's world and in his thought. Moreover, when Luther insisted that in an emergency any baptized person may forgive sins or baptize, he was thinking not of a priesthood of all believers but precisely of the necessity that the *public* office, ordained by Christ, *must* be filled. God's people must have God's word publicly in any and all situations. This is especially true of emergency baptisms, which were never conceived of as a private act. In fact, the privatization of the Christian faith has resulted in our misconstruing the spiritual priesthood we all share *in common* (not individually). I am especially grateful to Theo Dieter for demanding clarification of this point.

18. See "Predigtamt," in *Deutsches Wörterbuch*, ed. Jakob Grimm et al., 16 vols. (Leipzig: Hirzel, 1854–1960), 13:2084, "*Amt und Wirkungskreis eines Predigers.*"

19. See Philip Jakob Spener, *Pia desideria*, trans. Theodore Tappert (Philadelphia: Fortress Press, 1964), 92–95. See also, Philip Jakob Spener, *Der hochwichtige Articul von der Wiedergeburt . . . in sechs und sechzig Wochen-Predigten* (Frankfurt/Main: Zunner, 1715), 555–72.

20. Luther, too, in his explanation of the third article of the Creed, found in both the Large and Small Catechisms, made the same point. Faith is not a human work but the work of the Holy Spirit using the means of grace in the church. The fact that the Schwabach Articles do not use the term *Predigtamt* is an indication not that Melanchthon did not understand the word to mean the public office of the ministry, but rather that he made more specific that the "oral Word" used in those articles referred to the public office. Otherwise, why he would have introduced the term (and in the Latin, *ministerium*) at all?

21. Gerhard Forde, "The Ordained Ministry," in *Called and Ordained: Lutheran Perspectives on the Office of the Ministry*, ed. Marc Kolden and Todd Nichol (Minneapolis: Fortress Press, 1990), 117–36, here 133.

22. This is why in Ap 13 Melanchthon can entertain the notion that ordination, rightly understood, could be a sacrament. Here the comments of Werner Elert, *The Structure of Lutheranism* (St. Louis: Concordia, 1962), 339–351, are not always very helpful, although he does understand the way Pietism undermined the office (p. 362).

23. For a partisan view of the American fight in the nineteenth century, see Todd Nichol, "Ministry and Oversight in American Lutheranism," in Kolden and Nichol, eds., *Called and Ordained*, 93–113. For more on this issue, see chapters 1 and 2. Of course, a similar "transference" is argued by those who insist that only certain, historically successful bishops can transfer authority to an officeholder. We may place a person into an office, but it is the office, not our placing a person in it, that holds the authority.

24. This *Übertragungslehre* has recently been represented in a document produced for the VELKD (the People's Evangelical Lutheran Church in Germany). See "Allgemeines Priestertum, Ordination und Beauftragung nach evangelischem Verständnis—Eine Empfehlung der Bischofskonferenz der VELKD," *Evangelischer Pressedienst [epd] Dokumentation* 12/2005 (March 15, 2005): 5–23. It is so filled with errors that even Dorothea Wendebourg, the chair of the commission that produced it, rejected its conclusions. In fact, it is largely based upon

the work of Goertz and Härle, whose peculiar notions of the priesthood of all believers have dominated recent literature (especially the *RGG* and *TRE*). See my critique of their work in chapter 1. That the theological constructs from German Pietism should come, once again, to dominate Lutheran theology and Luther studies is unfortunate. Perhaps most questionable is the way in which the Lutheran Confessions become footnotes to a particular position in Luther studies and the way that other positions are simply dismissed by the authors without being taken seriously. (Thus, they invariably paraphrase [and thereby distort] CA 5's *Predigtamt* by using a word that is completely foreign to sixteenth-century German: *Verkündigungsamt*. The anti–Roman Catholic position on ordination and the public office of ministry has more in common with certain strands of Reformed thought than with either Luther or Lutheranism. For another current debate over ordination in Germany, see Henning Theißen, "Die Öffentlichkeit der Verkündigung: Zur Auseinandersetzung mit dem rheinischen Ordinationsgesetz," *Luther* 78 (2007): 18–31.

25. CA 14, in *BC 2000*, 47.

26. One interesting example of this misunderstanding occurred when George Lindbeck, a systematic theologian, analyzed this article at the celebration of the 450th anniversary of the Augsburg Confession in Augsburg, Germany. The subsequent public discussion included a host of prominent church historians who objected to his construal of the article. See George Lindbeck, "*Rite vocatus*: Der theologische Hintergrund zu CA 14," in *Confessio Augustana und Confutatio: Der Augsburger Reichstag 1530 und die Einheit der Kirche*, ed. Erwin Iserloh (Münster: Aschendorffsche Verlagsbuchhandlung, 1980), 454–72. A similar impasse occurred when Michael Root, a systematician, and Gerhard Forde, a church historian turned systematician, debated CA 7 at a convocation of teaching theologians. See Gerhard O. Forde, "Satis est? What Do We Do When Other Churches Don't Agree," and "'Satis Est': What Do We Do When Other Churches Don't Agree?," unpublished papers delivered at the 1990 Convocation for Teaching Theologians meeting in Techny, Illinois.

27. CA 14 (German), in *BC 2000*, 46. I am grateful to Pastor Kris Baudler for pointing out an error in CA 14, in *BC 2000*, 46, which has been rectified in subsequent printings. This citation reflects the textual history more accurately.

28. Ap 13.11, trans. Charles Arand, in *BC 2000*, 220.

29. Ap 13.7, in *BC 2000*, 220. The chief function of most priests in the late Middle Ages was to recite private masses on behalf of the dead. For statistics for Wittenberg, see Helmar Junghans, "Luther on the Reform of Worship," in *Harvesting Martin Luther's Reflections on Theology, Ethics and the Church*, ed. Timothy J. Wengert (Grand Rapids, Mich.: Eerdmans, 2004).

30. WATR 1:34 (no. 90), recorded by Veit Dietrich in November 1531.

31. This was one of the mistakes for which the church historians most faulted Lindbeck's analysis.

32. For example, the pulpit in the Foundation Church in Tübingen, built in the late fifteenth century, had the likenesses of these four encasing the pulpit, something Philip Melanchthon would have seen regularly in his days there as a student.

33. Cf. CA 28.53: ". . . ut res ordine in ecclesia gerantur" (German: damit es ordentlich in der Kirche zugehe . . .").

34. It should be noted that the preface to *The Book of Concord* does not forbid the proper use of the *Variata*, as Melanchthon's revisions came to be known. See the preface, par. 17, in *BC 2000*: 11 (BSLK 751, 37—752, 24).

35. *Melanchthon Briefwechsel: Texte*, vol. 6 (Stuttgart: Frommann-Holzboog, 2006), 470, 11–18 (no. 1640, October 4, 1535). The verb *ordre* is the sixteenth-century English word for "ordain."

36. See WA Br 11:155–57. For an English translation, see Timothy J. Wengert, "Certificate of Ordination (1545) for George von Anhalt, Coadjutor Bishop of Merseburg," *Lutheran Quarterly* 16 (2002): 229–33. The document was signed by Martin Luther, who presided at the consecration, and others. In his otherwise thorough analysis of ordination in Wittenberg, Martrin Krarup, *Ordination in Witteberg: Die Einsetzung in das kirchliche Amt in Kursachsen zur Zeit der Reformation* (Tübingen: Mohr Siebeck, 2007), never examines this document or Wittenberg's position regarding episcopal ordination by evangelical bishops.

37. Ap 12.125–30 already laid blame at the doorstep of one particular bishop, the papal legate Cardinal Campeggio, and his boss, Clement VII, bishop of Rome. See Timothy J. Wengert, "Philip Melanchthon's Last Word to Cardinal Lorenzo Campeggio, Papal Legate

at the 1530 Diet of Augsburg," in *Dona Melanchthoniana: Festgabe für Heinz Scheible zum 70. Geburtstag*, ed. Johanna Loehr (Stuttgart-Bad Cannstatt: Frommann-Holzboog, 2001), 457–83.

38. Robert Kolb, "Philipp Melanchthon: Reformer and Theologian," *Concordia Journal* 23 (1997): 309–16, esp. 313.

39. Cf. Henry Eyster Jacobs, *Historical Introduction, Appendixes and Indexes to the Book of Concord; or, the Symbolical Books of the Evangelical Lutheran Church* (Philadelphia, 1883), 110.

40. Ap 14.1, in *BC 2000*, 222–23.

41. Ibid.

42. Ibid. See also his comments appended to his signature in the Smalcald Articles (*BC 2000*, 326).

43. Ap 14, 2–3.

44. The only remaining exception is the Vatican itself.

45. This accident of medieval European history had to do with grants of large tracts of land by secular princes (especially the Holy Roman Emperor) to bishops, archbishops, and abbots. See CA 28.12 (German), in *BC 2000*, 92: "That is why one should not mix or confuse the two authorities, the spiritual and the secular."

46. CA 28.5 (German), in *BC 2000*, 92.

47. CA 28.21 (German), in: *BC 2000*, 94. The addition of the final phrase indicates that the *authority* of the office does not derive from election by the princely patron in the sixteenth century or by the synod assembly (for bishops) or the congregation (for pastors) in the twenty-first century.

48. CA XXVIII.34 (German), in *BC 2000*, 96. The examples Melanchthon furnished included to require certain actions to obtain grace, to attach sin to matters of *adiaphora* (already dealt with in CA 15), and, in short, to "ensnare consciences" (par. 42). He defined the gospel especially in CA 1–6 and 20.

49. CA 28.52 (German), in *BC 2000*, 98.

50. SA 3.10.1, in *BC 2000*, 323–24.

51. TPPP 66, in *BC 2000*, 340.

52. Throughout the Treatise (especially TPPP 61, 63, and 65), Melanchthon refers to *pastores*, which the German translation rendered *Pfarrherren*. This word in the sixteenth century did not designate all of the ordained, but rather that one person who was the head pastor in a church or town. Thus, in Wittenberg, the only *Pfarrherr* was

Johannes Bugenhagen. Later, ordination certificates were prepared by the university faculty or the local consistory and performed by bishops or superintendents. (After the Peace of Augsburg in 1555, it became nearly impossible for the evangelicals in the Holy Roman Empire to have bishops. However, several bishops signed the preface to *The Book of Concord* in 1580 [*BC 2000*, 15].)

53. I am indebted to Robert Kolb for this insight.

4. Bishops in the Augsburg Confession: Servants of the Crucified

1. Heiko Oberman, *Luther: Man between God and the Devil* (New Haven, Conn.: Yale University Press, 1989), xvii.

2. Merlyn E. Satrom, "Bishops and Ordination in the Lutheran Reformation of Sixteenth-Century Germany," *Lutheran Forum* 33, no. 2 (Summer 1999): 12–19.

3. Robert Goeser, "The Historic Episcopate and the Lutheran Confessions," *Lutheran Quarterly* 1 (1987): 214–32.

4. For a very different view, see chapter 3.

5. Ralph F. Smith, *Luther, Ministry, and Ordination Rites in the Early Reformation Church* (New York: Peter Lang, 1996).

6. *Nikolaus von Amsdorf als Bischof von Naumburg* (Gütersloh: Gerd Mohn, 1961).

7. For Luther's comments, see WA 53:219–60, *Exempel, einen rechten christlichen Bischof zu weihen*.

8. *TRE* 6:690–94.

9. Hans-Otto Wölber, "*Usus evangelii*: Das Bischofsamt in reformatorischer Sicht," in *Mensch und Meschensohn: Festschrift für Bischof Professor D. Karl Witte*, ed. Hartmut Sierig (Hamburg: Wittig, 1963), 81–98.

10. For Lutheran theologians, God uses the law, first, to maintain order and restrain evil in the world and, second, to reveal human sin and drive the sinner to Christ and the gospel. In the third use of the law (a term coined by Melanchthon in 1534 to combat those who either were making the gospel into new law or were arguing that the law did not apply at all in the Christian life), Christians, as believers, apply these two uses to themselves as forgiven sinners. See Timothy J. Wengert, *A Formula for Parish Practice* (Grand Rapids, Mich.: Eerdmans, 2006).

11. Bernhard Lohse, "The Development of the Offices of Leadership in the German Lutheran Churches: 1517–1918," in *Episcopacy in the*

Lutheran Church? Studies in the Development and Definition of the Office of Church Leadership, ed. Ivar Asheim and Victor R. Gold (Philadelphia: Fortress Press, 1970), 51–71.

12. *Amt und Ordination bei Luther und Melanchthon* (Göttingen: Vandenhoeck & Ruprecht, 1962). Lohse also misconstrues WA 53:253, 6–8.

13. James Estes, *Peace, Order and the Glory of God: Secular Authority and the Church in the Thought of Luther and Melanchthon, 1518–1559* (Leiden: Brill, 2005), 205–12.

14. Martin Brecht, ed., *Martin Luther und das Bischofsamt* (Berlin: Calwer Verlag, 1990).

15. See chapters 1 and 2 for substantiation of Brecht's point.

16. Heinz-Meinolf Stamm, "Luthers Berufung auf die Vorstellungen des Hieronymus vom Bischofsamt," in Brecht, ed., *Martin Luther*, 15–26.

17. Gottfried Krodel, "Luther und das Bischofsamt nach seinem Buch 'Wider den falsch genannten geistlichen Stand des Papstes und der Bischöfe,'" in Brecht, ed., *Martin Luther*, 27–65.

18. Martin Brecht, "Das Zusammenwirken des Bischofs mit der Gemeinde bei der Bestellung von Pfarrern und Predigern," in Brecht, 66–68.

19. Ibid.

20. Ken Miura and Martin Brecht, "De instituendis ministris—das Problem der Amtseinsetzungen bei den Böhmen," in Brecht, ed., *Martin Luther*, 69–72; *On the Instituted Ministries* and *That a Christian Assembly or Congregation Has the Right and Authority to Judge All Teaching* (WA 11:401–16 [LW 39:301–14]). See also chapter 2.

21. Markus Wriedt, "Luthers Gebrauch der Bischofstitulatur in seinen Briefen," in Brecht, ed., *Martin Luther*, 73–100.

22. Martin Brecht, "Die Visitation—Abdeckung eines Teilbereichs kirchenleitender Aufgaben," in Brecht, ed., *Martin Luther*, 101–4.

23. James Schaaf, "Der Landesherr als Notbischoff," in Brecht, ed., *Martin Luther*, 105–8.

24. Rolf Decot, "Luthers Kompromißvorschlag an die Bischöfe auf dem Augsburger Reichstag 1530," in Brecht, ed., *Martin Luther*, 109–19.

25. Martin Brecht, "Bemerkungen zur Ordination," in Brecht, ed., *Martin Luther*, 120–22.

26. Irmgard Höß, "Luther und die Bischofseinsetzungen in Merseburg und Kammin" and Hans-Ulrich Delius, "Das Naumburger Bischofexperiment und Martin Luther," in Brecht, ed., *Martin Luther*, 123–30 and 131–40, respectively. For more on von Amsdorf's tenure as bishop, see Peter Brunner, *Nikolaus von Amsdorf als Bischof von Naumburg: eine Untersuchung zur Gestalt des evangelischen Bischofamtes in der Reformationszeit* (Gütersloh: Mohn, 1961); Hans-Ulrich Delius, *Nikolaus von Amsdorf: Erster und einziger evangelischer Bischof von Zeitz* (Zeitz: Der Neue Weg, 1967); and Robert Kolb, *Nikolaus von Amsdorf (1483–1565): Popular Polemics in the Preservation of Luther's Legacy* (Nieuwkoop: De Graaf, 1978).

27. CA 28 is titled by Melanchthon "De vi ecclesiastica." Far from *not* defining the episcopal office but only its "authority," this title reflects Melanchthon's conviction that the meaning of a concept includes both what a thing is and what its power or effect is. Thus, in the first and subsequent editions of the *Loci Communes*, Melanchthon moves from "Quid sit evangelium" to "De vi evangelii." Thus, Melanchthon might rather be saying that because both sides agree that bishops, who practice oversight in the church, are important, the only question in the definition of bishops has to do with their power in the church.

28. Here Wilhelm Maurer's oft-cited position that the two are not connected rests upon a misunderstanding of the nature of the negotiations in Augsburg. See Wilhelm Maurer, *Historical Commentary on the Augsburg Confession*, trans. H. George Anderson (Philadelphia: Fortress Press, 1986), 64. For a more balanced view, see Gunther Wenz, *Theologie der Bekenntnisschriften der evangelisch-lutherischen Kirche*, 2 vols. (Berlin: de Gruyter, 1996–1997), 2:437–64.

29. For the Apology, see Charles Arand, "Melanchthon's Rhetorical Argument for *sola fide* in the Apology," *Lutheran Quarterly* 14 (2000): 280–308; and Timothy J. Wengert, "Philip Melanchthon's Last Word to Cardinal Lorenzo Campeggio, Papal Legate at the 1530 Diet of Augsburg," in: *Dona Melanchthoniana: Festgabe für Heinz Scheible zum 70. Geburtstag*, ed. Johanna Loehr (Stuttgart-Bad Cannstatt: Frommann-Holzboog, 2001), 457–83; for the Augsburg Confession, see Timothy J. Wengert, "The Rhetorical Key to the Lutheran Confessions for Faith and Life in Today's Church," *Seminary Ridge Review* 4, no. 2 (Spring 2002): 45–61.

30. Nicole Kuropka, *Philipp Melanchthon: Wissenschaft und Gesellschaft* (Tübingen: Mohr Siebeck, 2002), esp. 211–32. For all of Wilhelm Maurer's insights, he pays no attention whatsoever to the rhetorical structure of the article.

31. Thus, it takes on the form of an *objurgatio* more often used in the *genus demonstrativum*, the opposite of which was *laudatio*.

32. I am indebted to Charles Arand for this insight.

33. Only the second issue is dealt with by the so-called Torgau articles, and then only as an attack on the papacy.

34. Although not the source for this particular argument, Neoplatonism itself saw mixture as a sign of the fall into matter and complexity.

35. See CA 20.15–18, in *BC 2000*, 54–55, and especially the reference to Romans 5:1 in par. 16.

36. Cf. Luther's use of the term in WA 32:543, 30–31 (Sermons on Matthew 5–7; LW 21:293): "Da mustu mir nicht ein gemenge machen und die zwei [Verheißung und Verdienst] untereinander brewen." See also WA 12:398, 11–16 (Sermons on 1 Peter; LW 30:144), where Luther associates Babylon and, hence, Rome with an "unordentliches Gemenge"; WA 15:38, 27 (*To the City Councilmen of Germany*; LW 45:360); and finally, WA 29:98, 5 (Sermon on Laetare 1529), 34^2:502, 25–26 (Christmas Sermon 1531) and 51:241, 21–30 (*Exposition of Psalm 101*; LW 13:197), where his use of the term related directly to the confusion of the two governments. This information was gained by using *Luthers Werke im WWW* (ProQuest-CSA, 2000–2007).

37. Melanchthon purposely omitted the much more contested proof text from the so-called Torgau articles, Matthew 16:19. CA 28.5 reads: "Nun lehren die Unseren also, daß der Gewalt der Schlussel oder der Bischofen sei, lauts des Evangeliums, ein Gewalt und Befehl Gottes, das Evangelium zu predigen, die Sunde zu vergeben und zu behalten und die Sakrament zu reichen und handeln."

38. Melanchthon's inclination to move from the Aristotelian analytical question "Quid sit" to "Quid effectus" has been demonstrated by Peter Fraenkel, "Revelation and Tradition: Notes on Some Aspects of Doctrinal Continuity in the Theology of Philip Melanchthon," *Studia Theologica* (Lund) 13 (1959): 97–133; Siegfried Wiedenhofer, *Formalstrukturen humanistischer und reformatorischer Theologie bei Philipp*

Melanchthon, 2 vols. (Frankfurt: Peter Lang, 1976), 1:195ff., 215–233, and 370ff.; and Timothy J. Wengert, *Philip Melanchthon's* Annotationes in Johannem *in Relation to Its Predecessors and Contemporaries* (Geneva: Droz, 1987), 208–11. It allowed him to move seamlessly from the content of the gospel (justification by faith alone) to its effect (law and gospel).

39. German: "durch das Amt der Predig und durch die Handreichung der heiligen Sakrament." This definition implies that for Melanchthon the distinction between the offices of pastor and bishop would always be "de iure humano." God established a single *ministerium* to proclaim the gospel and administer the sacraments; human beings made distinctions within this *ministerium*, necessary for good order. The same point is made more directly in the so-called Torgau articles (BSLK 124, 31–33): "Item dieweil die Schlussel nicht anders sind, denn Evangelium predigen und Sakrament reichen, hat der Babst nicht mehr Gewalt durch die Schlussel dann ein jeder Pfarrner."

40. CA 28.21–22, in *BC 2000*, 95, emphasis added. In the German, Melanchthon added, "to preach the gospel," and stated, "That is why parishioners (*Pfarrleut*) and churches owe obedience to bishops." In Mittelhochdeutsch, the word *Pfarrmann* (plural: *Pfarrleut*) could mean either "pastor" or "parishioner." Melanchthon also uses a standard rhetorical ploy ("as they say") to indicate to the reader that this is not necessarily the language he would employ (he prefers "according to the gospel").

41. It appears, for example, on the title page of Jerome Emser's translation of the New Testament from 1527.

42. A consequence of the doctrine of the two estates (*Zwei-Stände Lehre*) discussed in chapter 1.

43. Here, the new English translation is not strong enough, translating the phrase "praeter haec" as simply "moreover." It meant, rather, "besides these things" (namely, pars. 5–29).

44. Eck's charges also contributed to the formulation of CA 20.

45. *Confutatio* is the Latin term for the Greek technical term *lusis*, the "refutation of an argument." See Aristotle, *Rhetoric* 2.25.9 (1402b, 23). In a rhetorical argument, one must only show that the opponents' conclusions are not necessarily true, which is precisely what Melanchthon set out to do here.

46. These were standard arguments, the last of which is found, among other places, in Thomas Aquinas, *S. T.* 2/2 q. 122 a. 4 ad 4.

47. See Wengert, "Philip Melanchthon's Last Word," 462.

48. CA 28.42, in *BC 2000*, 96–97 (emphasis added): doing manual labor on festivals, not praying the seven hours, not abstaining from certain foods, imagining that fasting pleases God or that sins in reserved cases could only be forgiven by the one who reserved the case.

49. CA 28.42 (Latin), in *BC 2000*, 97.

50. The others were Titus 1:14 and Matthew 15:13-14. The use of Colossians 2, which in verse 23, according to Melanchthon, introduced the distinction between the two kinds of righteousness, linked this section to the first. He provided a similar interpretation of the Colossians passage in Ap 15.22–37, in *BC 2000*, 227–28, linking it to the errant teaching of Roman bishops, who tied ceremonies to justification.

51. CA 28.49, in *BC 2000*, 98.

52. CA 28.53 (German), in *BC 2000*, 98: "for the sake of good order in the church, but not thereby to obtain God's grace, to make satisfaction for sin, or to bind consciences." Cf. CA 15.

53. See Ap 7/8.38–46, in *BC 2000*, 181–83, for more on the question of church practices.

54. In both the German and Latin of par. 64, Melanchthon used an ethical term favored by both Luther and him: *epieikeia* (Latin: *aequitas*; German: *Gleichmut*), but here in the German text glossed as *Linderung*.

55. In Ap 4.233–34, in *BC 2000*, 155, Melanchthon tied the need for episcopal flexibility directly to justification by faith.

56. But cf. pars. 1–4, which in some ways function to get the reader's attention. For the parts of a speech, see Cicero, *De Oratore*, 2.80: "Iubent enim exordiri ita, ut eum, qui audiat, benevolum nobis faciamus et docilem et attentum; deinde rem narrare, et ita ut veri similis narratio sit, ut aperta, ut brevis; post autem dividere causam aut proponere; nostra confirmare argumentis ac rationibus; deinde contraria refutare; tum autem alii conclusionem orationis et quasi perorationem conlocant, alii iubent, ante quam peroretur, ornandi aut augendi causa digredi, deinde concludere ac perorare." Aristotle, *Rhetoric* 3.19, defined the peroration as having four parts: (1) to make the audience well-disposed toward the speaker and ill-disposed to one's opponent, (2) to emphasize the leading facts of the case, (3) to cause the proper emotive response in the hearers, and (4) to refresh their memories. In this section, Melanchthon used the reference to Peter to do the first (par. 76). He then rehearsed the main

points, which also served to refresh the memory of the readers (par. 77). Finally, he used a powerful emotive conclusion by accusing the bishops of fostering schism (par. 78).

57. CA XXVIII.78, in *BC 2000*, 102. Melanchthon reminded the bishops of this charge three different times in the Apology: in Ap 12.125–130; 14.2, 5; and 28.5 and 25, in *BC 2000*, 208–9, 222–23, and 289 and 294, respectively.

58. See especially par. 23–28 and 34–56.

59. The word comes up in CA 28.4, 42, 49, 56, 64, 65, 68, and 77.

60. See, especially, CA 28.8, 30 (Latin), and 53, in *BC 2000*, 92, 95, and 98.

61. CA 28.30 in the Latin also used the phrase *episcopi seu pastores*.

5. Witnessing to the Evangelical Office of Bishop in *The Book of Concord*

1. Par. 9: "Do they merit forgiveness of sins? Are they acts of worship which God approves as righteousness? Do they make hearts alive?"

2. As noted in chapter 4, in a *confutatio*, the speaker or writer must show only that a (legal or, here, theological) text can have a different meaning from the opposition's construal.

3. See Timothy J. Wengert, "Martin Luther's Movement toward an Apostolic Self-Awareness as Reflected in His Early Letters," *Luther-Jahrbuch* 61 (1994): 71–92. The opponents' syllogism would read as follows. Major: obey your leaders (Hebrews 13:17); middle: we are your leaders; therefore obey us. Melanchthon introduced, via Galatians 1:8, a second syllogism that modifies the first. Major: all leaders must follow the gospel before being obeyed; minor: the present bishops are leaders who do not follow the gospel; therefore, they are not the leaders described in Hebrews 13 and thus cannot be obeyed.

4. For a brief description of these two versions, the latter of which is translated in *BC 2000*, see the editors' introduction there.

5. This may not be that far from true. For example, in the Peasants' War of 1525, the one area in South Germany that avoided revolt was the Kraichgau, an area comprised of virtually independent lesser lords who had cast their lot early on in favor of the Reformation.

6. Pindar, *Isthmionikai*, VII, 23, 24.

7. Remember that Melanchthon conceived this, like Article 28, in the judicial genre of speech.

8. TPPP, 32, in *BC 2000*, 335.

9. WA 9:677–715, with *Beilage* (appendix).

10. See James Estes, *Peace, Order and the Glory of God: Secular Authority and the Church in the Thought of Luther and Melanchthon, 1518–1559* (Leiden: Brill, 2005).

11. See the most recent discussion by Martin Krarup, *Ordination in Wittenberg: Die Einsetzung in das kirchliche Amt in Kursachsen zur Zeit der Reformation* (Tübingen: Mohr Siebeck, 2007), 85–120.

12. See pars. 67–71, where he mustered both biblical and patristic evidence.

13. See Forde, "The Ordained Ministry," in *Called and Ordained: Lutheran Perspectives on the Office of the Ministry*, ed. Todd Nichol and Marc Kolden (Minneapolis: Fortress Press, 1990), 133.

14. Par. 79: "Whereas the bishops, who are beholden to the pope, defend ungodly doctrine and ungodly worship and do not ordain godly teachers but abet the pope's violence instead; whereas, moreover, they have taken jurisdiction away from pastors and in tyrannical fashion exercise it alone; whereas, finally, in marital matters they enforce many unjust laws: therefore, these constitute many sufficient and necessary causes why the churches should not acknowledge them as bishops."

15. For more on this issue, see Gordon Lathrop and Timothy J. Wengert, *Christian Assembly* (Minneapolis: Fortress Press, 2004).

16. In the same way, teachers of the church exercise their God-given authority by teaching and preachers by preaching.

17. Of the 116 uses of this word in Luther's writings, see especially WA 8:685, 8–10 (*A Christian Admonition*; LW 45:70) and 49:313, 18 (cf. Lathrop and Wengert, *Christian Assembly*, 156).

Concluding Thoughts

1. For a far more extensive discussion of this point, see Gordon Lathrop, *The Pastor: A Spirituality* (Minneapolis: Fortress Press, 2006).

2. WA 31^1:199–200.

Index

BX 8065.3 .W46 2008
Wengert, Timothy J.
Priesthood, pastors,
bishops